PAUL D. SANSONE, O.F.M.

NTOA 2

Weinfeld • The Organizational Pattern and the Penal Code
of the Qumran Sect

NOVUM TESTAMENTUM ET ORBIS ANTIQUUS (NTOA)

Im Auftrag des Biblischen Instituts
der Universität Freiburg Schweiz
herausgegeben von Max Küchler
in Zusammenarbeit mit Gerd Theissen

About the author:

Moshe Weinfeld, born in 1925, received all his degrees (BA, MA and PhD) at the
Hebrew University of Jerusalem and is Professor of Biblical Studies there. He
served as visiting Professor at the Jewish Theological Seminary of America (1967–
1969), at Brandeis University (1968) and at University of California, San Diego
(1981).
He is editor of *Shnaton – An Annual for Biblical and Ancient Near Eastern
Studies*, serves at the Editorial Board of *Vetus Testamentum*, and was nominated
honorary member of the Society for Biblical Literature in America. Apart from
articles in the field of Bible and the Ancient Near East his works include:
Studies in the Historiography of the Former Prophets, Jerusalem 1966.
Deuteronomy and the Deuteronomic School, Oxford 1972.
Mesopotamian Creation Epic – enuma elish, Transliteration, Translation and
    Notes, Jerusalem 1973.
*Justice and Righteousness in Israel in the light of Near Eastern Concepts of
    Justice*, Jerusalem 1985.

NOVUM TESTAMENTUM ET ORBIS ANTIQUUS   2

Moshe Weinfeld

The Organizational Pattern and the Penal Code of the Qumran Sect

A Comparison with Guilds and Religious Associations
of the Hellenistic-Roman Period

ÉDITIONS UNIVERSITAIRES FRIBOURG SUISSE
VANDENHOECK & RUPRECHT GÖTTINGEN
1986

CIP-Kurztitelaufnahme der Deutschen Bibliothek

Weinfeld, Moshe:

The organizational pattern and the penal code of the
Qumran sect: a comparison with guilds and religious
associations of the Hellenistic-Roman period. / Weinfeld,
Moshe.
Fribourg (Suisse): Editions Universitaires
Göttingen: Vandenhoeck und Ruprecht, 1986

(Novum testamentum et orbis antiquus; 2)
ISBN 3-7278-0363-0 (Editions Universitaires)
ISBN 3-525-53901-0 (Vandenhoeck und Ruprecht)
NE: GT

Druckvorlage auf IMB Compocart durch die wissenschaftliche Sekretärin
des Biblischen Instituts Freiburg Schweiz, Bernadette Schacher

Veröffentlicht mit der Unterstützung des Hochschulrates
der Universität Freiburg Schweiz

© 1986 by Universitätsverlag Freiburg Schweiz
Paulusdruckerei Freiburg Schweiz
ISBN 3-7278-0363-0 (Universitätsverlag)
ISBN 3-525-53901-0 (Vandenhoeck und Ruprecht)

TABLE OF CONTENTS

5

6

INTRODUCTION

H. Bardtke was the first to draw attention to the similarities between the organization of the Qumran sect and contemporaneous Hellenistic associations (1). W. Tyloch continued his line of investigation (2). However, no detailed comparative investigation of the rules and legal structure of the Qumran community has been done so far. In this study I shall endeavor to make up at least some of the deficit and by means of a detailed analysis will strive to show that the organizational pattern of the Qumran sect, and likewise the penal code contained in 1QS are congruent with those of the cultic associations of Ptolemaic Egypt as well as of other regions of the Hellenistic and Roman world.

It should be stated however that our conclusion does not at all affect the nature and character of the sect as such. Our sole concern is the formal structure of the religious sect. In this respect the problem under discussion is similar to that of the covenant in recent OT research. As is well known, from the point of view of terminology and structure the covenant between God and Israel, as well as between God and the Patriarchs and the Davidic dynasty, has its parallels in the political treaties and royal commitments of the ancient Near East (3). But this does not affect in any measure the uniqueness of the concept *berit* in the religion of Israel.

------

1   "Die Rechtstellung der Qumran Gemeinde", *ThLZ* 86 (1961), 93-104; *idem*, *Theol. Rundschau* 33 (1968) 217-236; compare C. Schneider, "Zur Problematik des Hellenistischen in den Qumrantexten", *Qumranprobleme*, ed. H. Bardtke, 1963, 299-344; M. Delcor, "Repas cultuels esséniens et thérapeutes, thiases et ḥaburoth", *Rev. Qumran* 6 (1968), 401-425; H. Mantel, "The Nature of the Great Synagogue", *HThR* 60 (1967), 69-91 analyzed the term *keneset ha-gedolah* against the background of the Hellenistic synods and reached the conclusion that the *keneset ha-gedolah* was a big synod consisting of local branches, but this is hardly convincing (cf. also E.E. Urbach, The Sages, p.944, n.87). Though it is true that the term *keneset* may be rendered "guild" or "association" (compare Akkadian *kiništu* and see note 79 in my article in *Tarbiz* 41 (1972), p. 359 and it indeed serves as an appellation for the Sect : כנסת אנשי היחד, 4QPB 6, J. Allegro, *JBL* 75 (1956), 174ff.; cf. also כנסת // עצה in כנסתם ונפרדה כנסתם אשר תובד עצתם, (4QPNah III : 7, *DJD* V, p. 39), *keneset ha-gedolah* is altogether different. The latter denotes a body which consists of national representatives, compare 1 Macc. 14:28 : "at a great assembly (συναγωγὴ μεγάλη = כנסת הגדולה) of priests, chiefs of the nation and elders". To my opinion, *keneset ha-gedolah* is analogous to the Egyptian "great *qnbt*" — great council which consists of the representatives of all the authorities : mayor, high priest, secretary of the state, etc. The great *qnbt* functioned also in a judicial capacity; for the great *qnbt* see P.M. Lurje, *Studien zum altägyptischen Recht* 1971, pp. 40ff.
2   *Aspekty Społeczne Gminy z Qumran*, Warsaw, 1968.
3   See my article "ברית" in *Theologisches Wörterbuch zum AT* (ed. Botterweck-Ringgren), vol. I, col. 782-808.

The same applies to the Qumran sect. Although the external form and structure of this sect is similar to that of the Hellenistic associations, the basic ideology of the sect is in its nature unique. The Qumran society considers itself as "a holy house of Israel בית קדש לישראל (1QS 8:5f.) or as "a council of the Holy of Holies of Aaron" סוד קודש קדשים לאהרן (*ibid.* 8:8f.), "a house of perfection and truth in Israel" בית תמים ואמת בישראל (*ibid.*, 8:9), etc., concepts which in a sense continue the Old Testament ideals of a holy nation and priestly kingdom (Ex. 19:6, 22:30, Deut. 7:6, 14:2, etc.). Moreover, the uniqueness is reflected not only in ideology but also in procedure : the way of commitment and the taking of the pledge. The ceremony of entering the covenant accompanied by blessings and curses as described in 1QS 1:16f. actually proceeds along the line of the ancient Shechemite covenant as presented in Deut. 27:12-13 (compare Jos. 8:30ff.). By the same token the declarations proclaimed in this ceremony : the recital of God's grace on the one hand (*ibid.* 21-22) and the confession of the sins of Israel on the other (lines 22-26), resemble the confession in Neh 9:6ff. which also contains a review of God's past grace on the one hand and self-condemnation (vv. 33f.) on the other. The confession in Nehemiah, like the one in the *Serekh*, joins the pledge of the people to keep the law (chap. 10).

One has to be aware therefore of the specific Jewish nature of the Qumran group, but this should not deter us from examining the external form of the Qumran organization against the background of cultic associations in this period in the vicinity.

Before we start our investigation our view of the nature of the Qumran documents involved (the Serekh) should be made clear. We accept in principle the opinion that the Manual of Discipline is the product of gradual literary development (cf. e.g. J. Murphy-O'Connor, *RB* 76 (1969), pp. 519ff.) though it is impossible — in our view — to draw an exact scheme of this development. We are convinced however that columns V-VII of 1 QS reflect the legal constitution of the sect, and as such resemble very much the legal codes of the various associations and sects discussed in our study.

The following are the codes cited in this book :

1. The code of the Labyads in Delphi (3rd Century B.C.E.), Dittenberger, *Sylloge,* II/2, 438.
2. A Demotic code from the days of Ptolemy III (223 B.C.E.), F. de Cenival, *Les associations religieuses en Egypte, d'après les documents démotiques,* 1972, Papyrus Lille 29, pp. 1-38.
3. A Demotic code from the days of Ptolemy VI (179 B.C.E.), F. Cenival, *op. cit.,* Pap. Caire 31178, pp. 39-44.
4. A Demotic code from the days of Ptolemy VI (157 B.C.E.), F. Cenival, *op. cit.,* Pap. Caire 30606, pp. 45-58.
5. A Demotic code from the days of Ptolemy VI (151 B.C.E.), F. Cenival, *op. cit.,* Pap. Hamburg, pp. 59-61.
6. A Demotic code from the days of Ptolemy VI (147 B.C.E.), F. Cenival, *op. cit.,* Pap. Caire 31179, pp. 63-72.
7. A Demotic code from the days of Ptolemy VIII (145 B.C.E.), F. Cenival, *op. cit.,* Pap. Caire 30605, pp. 73-81.
8. A Demotic code from the days of Ptolemy VIII (137 B.C.E.), F. Cenival, *op. cit.,* Pap. Prague, pp. 83-91.
9. A Demotic code from the days of Ptolemy VIII (137 B.C.E.), F. Cenival, *op. cit.,* Pap. Caire 30619, pp. 93-102.
10. A Demotic code from the days of Ptolemy Soter II (110-107 B.C.E.), F. Cenival, *op. cit.,* Pap. Berlin 3115, pp. 103-135.
11. A Greek code of the guild of Zeus Hypsistos in Egypt (69-58 B.C.E.), *HThR* 29 (1936), pp. 39ff.
12. A Greek code of a religious association from the days of Tiberius from Egypt; Husselman, Boak, Edgerton, Michigan *Papyri from Tebtunis* II, 1944, no. 243, pp. 90-100.
13. A Greek code from Egypt (43 C.E.), Husselman, Boak, Edgerton, *Papyri from Tebtunis* II, no. 244, pp. 100-109.
14. A thiasos of Palmyre (First Cent. C.E.), M.J. Teixidor, "Le Thiase de Belastro et de Beelshamèn", *CRAIBL* Avril-Juin 1981, pp. 306-314.
15. Attic Club (2nd Cent.C.E.), A.E. Raubitschek, "A New Attic Club (ERANOS)", *The J. Paul Getty Museum Journal* 9 (1981), pp. 93-98.
16. The Statutes of the Iobacchi (2nd Cent. C.E.), Dittenberger, *Sylloge/3,* no. 1109.
17. A list of members in the association of the Bacchi (2nd cent. C.E.), F. Cumont, "La grande inscription bacchique", *American Journal of Archaeology* 37 (1933), pp. 232ff.

I. The appellations סרך, יחד and רבים

The original meaning of סרך is "bond" or "cord" (4) and is to be compared with חבל "rope/cord" which likewise designates a guild or association : חבל נביאים (1 Sam. 10:5, 10) (5). The same applies to חבר whose original meaning is "binding" and "joining together" but also connotes an association or collegium such as חבר כהנים (Hos. 6:9), חבר הצרפים "guild of goldsmiths" (Neh. 3:8) (6) and חבר היהודים which appears on coins from the second Temple period (7) (cf. also חבר עיר in Rabbinic literature).

------

4   B. Levine ("Aramaic Texts from Persepolis", *JAOS* 92 (1972), 72ff.) associates *serekh* with Aramaic *sarakh* —— "head, officer" (Dan. 6:3-5 and Targums) and following this etymology understands the Qumran *serekh* as "rule, command" (authorized by a ruler or commander), cf. also L.H. Schiffman, *The Halakah at Qumran*, 1975, pp. 60-68. Levine admits that the basic meaning of *srk* in Biblical and Rabbinic usage is "to tie, adhere, follow", etc., but he postulates for *srk* a second meaning derived from Persian *sara* —— "head" (cf. F. Rosenthal, *A Grammar of Biblical Aramaic*, 1963, p. 58, rule 189) which connotes to his opinion "rule" or "administration", and concludes that the Qumran *serekh* is to be understood according to this meaning. Furthermore, he explains the verbal form of *srk* such as יסרוכו (1QM 2:1, 6) and סורכי המחנות (1QM 7:1) as denominative from סָרֶךְ "head". One has to admit that the Aramaic סרך "head, officer" seems to be a loanword from Persian *sara* but there is no necessity to derive the Qumran noun *serekh* and the verb *sarakh* from Persian *sara*. It could be well explained as derived from the basic meaning of *srk* "to tie, adhere", etc. as will be shown by us below.

5   Compare *ḥbl* (flock) of birds (*ʿṣrm*) in CTA 4 VII:57 (restored according to CTA 8:10ff.), and also "flock (*ḥbl*) of birds (*dʾiym*)" in CTA 19:33 (compare 18 IV:31) and also *ḥbl kṯrt* (CTA 11:6). This term in a prophetic context was discovered in a Southern Arabic inscription from Sheba. There we read : הוצת כל גום דאלם ... וחבלם, Rhodokanakis, *Altsabäische Texte* I (SBWA, Phil. hist. Kl. 206), 1927, p. 39; and also Rhodokanakis and M. Höfner, *Wiener Zeitschr. Kunde Morg.* 57 (1954), pp. 80ff. This should be translated : "(the *mukarib* = the priest) founded (literally : "grouped") the community of the gods... and the bond..." (on גום in the meaning of "confederation" or "community" compare in Phoenician and Punic inscriptions : *gw* (= κοινόν in a bilingual text; see Donner-Röllig, *KAI* 60:2, 5, 7, 8). According to Höfner and Rhodokanakis the text deals with the priest who establishes a covenant between the god and his worshippers (compare the role of Moses in the covenant between the Lord and Israel and also Jehoiada, 2 Kgs. 11).

6   Compare *ḥibrum* in Mari which like Hebrew חבר (cf. חבר הקיני in Jud. 4:11) means a tribal unit, an association of tribal families, see A. Malamat, *JAOS* 82 (1962), pp. 144-145. חבר denotes also a mercantile guild as may be learned from the use of *ḥbr* in the Egyptian tale of Wen-Amon (I, line 59, II, line 1) as well as from Job 40:30 (כנענים // חברים) and 2 Chr. 20:35-36, see B. Mazar, *The Israel Academy of Sciences and Humanities, Proceedings*, vol. I, no. 7 (1964), pp. 2-3; cf. also in the Damascus Covenant (13:15) : ואל יעש איש חבר למקח וממכר כי אם הודיע למבקר אשר במחנה ועשה אמנה "and let no one make a trade partnership unless he informs the overseer in the camp and makes an agreement".

7   Compare *ḥbr* in the Punic inscription from Marseilles (*KAI* 69:19) and see U. Rappaport, "On the meaning of *Heber ha-Yehudim*", *Studies in the History of the Jewish People and the Land of Israel*, vol. 3 (eds. U. Rappaport, A. Shochat,

Etymologically סרך equals שרך in classical Hebrew which means "twist" (Jer. 2:23) or "twisted thread" (8) and hence "strap" (cf. שרוך נעל, Gen. 14:23, Isa. 5:27 = shoelace). Similarly srk in Syriac and in the Rabbinic sources means "to tie", "adhere", "follow" (9). Arabic šrk as well connotes binding as well as establishing partnership, etc. By the same token Akkadian riksu and Hittite išḫiul which literally mean "bond", actually designate treaty, imposed obligation, etc. (10). סרך should therefore be likewise understood as "bond" in the sense of the binding rules (= the code) (11) of the sect as well as the sect based on these rules (12). This duplicity of meaning is found also in the concept ברית in the Qumran scrolls, which indicates both the *obligation* and the *organization* which is founded on the basis of the obligation (13). The German "Bund" also serves in these two meanings.

The fact that *serekh* also means a military order (cf. 1QM) does indeed support our supposition about the etymology of the word. The acts of binding and putting together in order are expressed in the ancient Semitic languages by identical verbs. Thus *(riksa) rakāsu* in Akkadian which literally means "to bind (a bond)" has the following meanings : 1) to impose an obligation or establish an agreement (14), 2) to set the

---

J. Shatzmiller), University of Haifa 1974 (Hebrew), pp. 59-67, who rightly claims that *Heber ha-Yehudim* indicates a body which incorporates the whole national sovereignty and not the representative or council. חבר here is parallel to יחד in the writings of the Qumran sect, thus we find in the Damascus Covenant "the עצת חבור ישראל" (12:8) comparable to "עצת היחד" in other writings of the sect.

8 שרוך (נעל) relates to the verb שרך like פתיל "cord" (Ex. 28:28, 37, Num. 15:38, Jud. 16:9 etc.) to פתל "twist".

9 Cf. B. Levine, *JAOS* 92 (1972), 72f. According to my opinion סרך בתה (B. Nidah 76b) is to be understood as the *daughter's following* (her mother's example) and the same applies to סרך תרומה (B. Hulin 106b) which means (washing before the secular meal) *following* (the example of) *Terumah*, and is derived from the basic meaning of סרך "to tie, adhere and follow" (see note 4).

10 The same applies to ברית. Cf. my article "ברית" in *ThWAT* I, 781-808 = *Theological Dictionary of the Old Testament* II, 253-279, and the references there.

11 As for example in 1QS 5:1 : "This is the סרך for the men of the community who devote themselves", which means : this is the *code* of the members of the sect, etc. In the Damascus Covenant פרוש interchanges with סרך (compare 12:19, 22 סרך מושב with 14:17 פרוש מושב) and means like סרך legal order or code (cf. L.H. Schiffman, *The Halakha at Qumran*, pp. 38f.). Such also is the meaning of פירוש in the Musaf prayer of the Sabbath (*SPB*, p. 229) : צוית פירושיה עם סידורי נסכיה "You commanded its legal specification with the *regulations* of its libations".

12 Compare for example אנשי הסרך "the men of the *Serekh*" (1QM 7:1), זקני הסרך "elders of the *Serekh*" (ibid. 13:1) which means the men or elders of the sectarian group, see the discussion of Y. Yadin, *The War of the Sons of Light and the Sons of Darkness*, pp. 148-150.

13 Cf. Also M.Z. Kaddari, *Semantic Fields in the Language of the Dead Sea Scrolls*, 1968, pp. 93-94 (Hebrew).

14 See Weidner, *AfO* 17 (1914-1916), 257ff. (*passim*), compare *riksa dunnunu* "to strengthen the bond = to validate the vassal oath" in connection with the vassal treaties; see my article in : *Maarav - A Journal for the study of the Northwest Semitic Languages and Literatures,* III (1982) pp. 46ff., note 95.

sacrifice in order (15) (compare *paššura rakāsu* (16) "to set a table" = ערך שלחן), 3) to draw up a military formation (17).

Hebrew ערך has the same range of meanings : 1) ערך ברית = to arrange an agreement/obligation (2 Sam. 23:5), 2) ערך העולה "set up the burnt offering" (Lev. 6:5); ערך ערך השלחן (18) "set the table order" (Ex. 40:4, 23), compare מערכה in Rabbinic literature (Mish.Yoma 4:6), 3) ערך מלחמה "draw the battle order" (Judg. 20:22, 1 Sam. 17:8, etc.) and compare מערכה "battle" (*passim*). In the light of this range of meanings סורכי המחנות (1QM 7:1) should be understood as עורכי מלחמה (1 Chr. 12:33) and ערכי מערכה (*ibid*. v. 38; עדרי is a corruption of ערכי, see various Hebrew manuscripts and the versions), i.e. the ones who array the military formation. The verb אסר "bind" has an identical range of meanings : 1) אסר אסר in Num. 30:4 like Akkadian *riksa rakāsu* means to assume an obligation and the same applies to אסר in Aramaic : לתקפה אסר "to strengthen the bond (= obligation)" in Dan. 6:8 is paralleled by קימה קים "establish a decree" and in the Aramaic Antiochus Scroll (19) we similarly read that the Hasmoneans "pledged a pledge" קיימו קיימא and "bound a bond" אסרו אסרא (v. 63) to celebrate the Hanukkah festival (20). 2) אסר in connection with arraying the battle order is found in 1 Kgs. 20:14, 2 Chr. 13,3 and in the War Scroll : תאסר המערכה "the battle order will be arrayed" (1QM 5:3) (21). The same range of meanings may be observed in the verb קשר : 1) קשר קשר means to conspire, actually to form an alliance against somebody (1 Kgs. 16:20, 2 Kgs. 12:21, etc.) (22) but it is also found in Mishnaic Hebrew in connection with arraying battle : קשרי מלחמה (Sotah 8:5) (23). The

---

15 For references cf. W. von Soden, *Akk. Handw.*, p. 946, 13)a.

16 *Ibid.*, 12)b.

17 *Ibid.*, p. 985 B 4); p. 946 12)c, p. 947 Gt 1). Compare also with other verbs for binding : *kaṣāru, ṣamādu (Enuma eliš* : II:2,4) in a military context.

18 ערך ערך overlaps formally *riksa rakāsu.*

19 See A.J. Wertheimer, *Batei Midrashot* I, 1968, p. 329 (Hebrew). For the antiquity of the scroll and its language see M.Z. Kaddari, *Leshonenu* 23 (1958), 129-146.

20 Compare 1 Macc. 4:59 : "Judas and his brothers and the entire assembly of Israel decreed/pledged (ἔστησεν) (to observe the festival)". Cf. Esther 9:27 (comp. vs. 21) : קימו וקבל "they took a pledge upon themselves", see *UF* 8 (1976), p. 411.

21 See Y. Yadin, *The Scroll of the War*, etc., p. 154. In the Targums this is rendered by טקס, (יאסר מלחמה = יטקוס קרבא). תעודה in connection with war and military formation (cf. Yadin, *ibid.*, 78ff.) belongs to the same semantic field and seems to derive from עוד "bind" as in Ps. 119:61 : חבלי רשעים עודני. For תעודה and its derivation see H. Yalon, *Studies in the Dead Sea Scrolls* (Philological Essays 1949-1952) Jerusalem 1967, pp. 85-86 (Hebrew).

22 Yadin, *The Scroll of the War*, etc., pp. 132ff. Compare Ps. 31:21 "(you protect them) מרכסי איש = from a conspiring alliance". רכס means "bind" like Akkadian *rakāsu*.

23 Cf. note 17 above for the same in Akkadian.

root סדר which occurs often in the War Scroll of Qumran (24) and is very common in Mishnaic Hebrew also belongs to the same semantic field. It is applied to the cult (סדר מערכה, BS 50:14, M. Tamid 2:4f.) as well as to military formations. סדר actually replaces classical Hebrew ערך although the root has its incipits in the Bible (25) in connection with a military array : והבא אל השדרות יומת "Whoever breaks through the ranks shall be killed" (2 Kgs. 11:8).

One has to admit however that although the etymology of סרך can be explained on the basis of cognate roots, the word סרך in its covenantal designation is not found in Hebrew besides Qumran. It seems to us therefore that this word was coined intentionally to serve as a substitute for the common Hellenistic term for an association : τάξις. Indeed, the term τάξις occurs as a translation of סרך in an ancient text of the Testament of Levi (26). It is derived from τάσσω "to arrange in order" and has a range of meanings similar to that of סרך : 1) a set of rules, 2) a military unit, 3) a political or religious association (27). The term סרך as an appellation for the sectarian covenant has to be seen therefore against the background of the Greek term τάξις prevalent in that period.

Another Greek term may also have contributed to the choice of *serekh*, and that is σπεῖρα which like τάξις denotes a tactical unit as well as a religious guild (28). Literally it is equivalent to שרוך > סרך since it too denotes a twisted thread (rope, cord, etc.).

יחד —— As a term for a community it appears only in the Qumran scrolls (29). The diffusion of the term in the literature of the sect is comparable to that of the parallel Greek term κοινόν or κοινωνία among terms for associations in the Hellenistic period (30). It seems that the term יחד was adopted by the sect under the influence of the Greek term κοινόν, κοινωνία which was commonly used at that time (31). Indeed,

---

24 Yadin, *The Scroll of the War*, etc., p. 133.
25 A fact overlooked by Yadin who says that the term is not attested in the OT (*ibid.*, p. 133). Just as Biblical שרוך becomes סרך in post-Biblical literature so Biblical שדר becomes סדר in post-Biblical times.
26 R.M. Charles, *The Greek Versions of the Testaments of the Twelve Patriarchs*, 1908, p. 250.
27 See Y. Yadin, *War Scroll*, pp. 137-139.
28 Cf. G. Quandt, *De Baccho ab Alexandri aetate in Asia Minore culto*, Halle 1912, pp. 242ff.
29 Note especially יחד with the article *ha-yaḥad* and cf. Dombrowski, "היחד and τὸ κοινόν", *HThR* 59 (1966), pp. 293ff. On the origins of this expression in the Bible see S. Talmon, *VT* 3 (1953), pp. 133ff. and also H. Yalon, *Studies in the Dead Sea Scrolls*, 1967, pp. 39-40, n. 35 (Hebrew).
30 On τὸ κοινόν see F. Poland, *Geschichte des griechischen Vereinswesens*, 1909, pp. 163ff.; E. Ziebarth, *Das Griechische Vereinswesen*, 1896, p. 136. The identity of κοινωνία, κοινόν with יחד was discussed by A. Dupont-Sommer, *Nouveaux aperçus sur les manuscrits de la Mer Morte*, 1953, p. 93; Th. Gaster, *The Dead Sea Scriptures*, 1956, p. 328; F.M. Cross, *The Ancient Library of Qumran*, 1961, p. 80, n. 43. See also Dombrowski, *HThR* 59 (1966), 293ff.

both Philo and Josephus speak of κοινόν and κοινωνία in the course of their descriptions of the life of the Essenes (*Quod omnis probus liber sit* 84, 91; *Bel. Jud.* II, 122, 123).

The concept of יחד may be illuminated by the term κοινωνία in Acts 2:42 (compare below on 1 Corinthians 10:16ff.). There we read about the organization of the Christian community in Jerusalem, which perseveres in the teaching (διδαχή) of the Apostles and practices the κοινωνία. The continuation of the passage speaks of the cooperation between the believers (ἐπὶ τὸ αὐτὸ εἶχον ἅπαντα κοινά) (32), the joint ownership of property and also worship in one accord (compare Acts 4:32). This cooperation calls to mind what is said of the יחד community : "This is the rule for the men of the community (אנשי היחד) who devote themselves to turn away from every evil ... to form a community (להיות ליחד) with respect to Torah and property" (1QS 5:1-2). As in the passage from Acts here also we find the יחד as a group observing the rules of Torah and of the division of property with the purpose "to be a יחד", i.e. to establish full unity (comp. 2:24). Both the κοινωνία in Acts and the יחד in the scroll of the sect entail a social-organizational and moral-religious significance (33). As we shall see, mutual aid and social morality comprised an important factor of the guilds and associations of those days.

רבים —— This term is identical with יחד in its meaning (34), and has rightly been compared to the Greek πλῆθος (35) which also indicates a guild or association (36). However, the more exact parallel term is οἱ πολλοί, which literally renders רבים, and relates to the community itself as a whole and not just to its representatives. Josephus, in describing the Essenes, tells us that they listen to the elders on the one hand, and

---

31 Cf. recently, M. Hengel, "Qumran und der Hellenismus", *Qumran, sa piété, sa théologie et son milieu*, ed. M. Delcor, 1978, 348ff. It is possible that יחד came to replace both the term חבר which was common among the Hasmoneans (see note 7) and the term חבורה which was prevalent among the Pharisees. The only exception is עצת חבור ישראל in CD 12:8 (cf. also 13:15, 14:16) and it may be that in this matter as in others there were differences between the Damascus sect and that of Qumran.

32 ἐπὶ τὸ αὐτό translate in the Septuagint יחד, and the Aramaic word behind this idiom is כחדא, see M. Black, *An Aramaic Approach to the Gospels and Acts/3*, 1966, pp. 233-257.

33 On this issue see J.A. Fitzmyer, *Essays on the Semitic Background of the New Testament*, 1971, pp. 283-284 (= *Essays Presented in Honor of Paul Schubert*, 1966, pp. 233-257).

34 רבים as an appellation of the sect is discussed by S. Lieberman, *JBL* 71 (1952), p. 203. On the congruence with יחד see H. Yalon (above n. 29), and also J. Licht, *Megilat HaSerakhim*, 1965, p. 109.

35 See Fitzmyer, *Essays*, pp. 290-291. πλῆθος meaning the community at large is prominent in Acts 6:2, 5, 19:9. A Similar situation exists in the Egyptian guilds, see Pap. Michigan 244:7 (below n.112).

36 On this expression in the Hellenistic communities see F. Poland, *Vereinswesen*, p. 168; Bauer, Arndt, Gingrich, *Lexicon of the NT*, p. 674, *s.v.* πλῆθος 2d.

to the πλείονες (= רבים) on the other (*Bel. Jud.* II, 146) (37). Especially instructive for our discussion is the passage in the Epistle to the Corinthians 10:16ff., which deals with κοινωνία (= יחד) and οἱ πολλοί (= רבים) in the context of a community meal (cup of blessing and breaking of bread) : οὐχὶ κοινωνία τοῦ σώματος τοῦ Χριστοῦ ἐστιν ... ἓν σῶμα οἱ πολλοί ἐσμεν. Paul declares that the bread and the wine over which they bless at the meal of the κοινωνία (= יחד) and the οἱ πολλοί (= רבים) are the body and blood of Jesus, and this is what makes the group "to be one" (see above). And this is in contrast to the worldly (κατὰ σάρκα) group which eats the flesh of sacrifices in the κοινωνία of the altar (on this issue and its connection with the מרזח (38) see below). Also in the Epistle to the Romans 12:4-5 we find the term οἱ πολλοί in an identical context.

רבים in the meaning of an organized public has been preserved in Rabbinic literature, especially in Mishnah Kiddushin 4:5 : שוטרי הרבים, and also in a Baraitha in Jer. Kiddushin 4:5, 76a (39). שוטרי הרבים are those who serve the public, in contrast to שוטרי הדיינים (Tosephta Sanhedrin 3:9), who serve in the courts only (40). In B. Yebamoth 86b, in a citation from an unknown source, we find : שוטרי הרבים בראשיכם (41). This source is apparently close in character to the sectarian sources which we are discussing.

A term similar to that of רבים is *mš'* found in the Demotic codes of the guilds from the Ptolemaic period, and means like רבים the multitude or the people (42). As will be seen below, *mr mš'* in these codes is comparable to the title of "the officer in charge of the רבים" (הפקיד בראש הרבים) found in the Manual of Discipline (6:14).

The three appellations of the sect סרך, יחד and רבים which are so typical to the sect's writings and which are not found in any other Second Temple period literature, reflect to my opinion the terms for groups and sects which were prevalant in the Hellenistic world :

1) τάξις, τάγμα, σπεῖρα (= סרך)
2) κοινόν, κοινωνία (= יחד)
3) οἱ πολλοί, πλῆθος (= רבים).

-----

37 Josephus referring to the Essenes in *Ant. Jud.* 18:22 mentions πλείστοις, but the reading there is disputed. See L.H. Feldmann, *Josephus*, IX, Loeb Classical Library, 1965, pp. 20-21, *n.a.*

38. Cf. H. Gressmann, *ZNW* 20 (1921), pp. 224-230.

39 מניין לרבות שוטרי הרבים וגבאי צדקה וסופרי דיינין ומכין
ברצועה ת"ל "מקרב אחיך תשים עליך מלך".

40 On שוטרי הדיינין as comparable to סופרי הדיינין see my discussion in "Judge and Officer in Ancient Israel and in the Ancient Near East", *Israel Oriental Studies* 7 (1977), p. 85.

41 See L. Ginsberg, *An Unknown Jewish Sect* (translated from the German edition of 1922), 1976, p. 49, n. 137.

In contrast to the Pharaisees who did not balk from using Greek terms for national institutions (cf. for example, *synédrion*), the members of the Qumran sect insisted on Hebrew terms and introduced for this purpose new terms in order ot avoid the usage of foreign words.

II. The Council

At the head of the *yaḥad* (43) we find a council of twelve men and three priests (44) who are "to perform truth, righteousness and justice" לעשות אמת וצדקה ומשפט (1QS 8:1-2), to be "true witnesses in judgment" עדי אמת למשפט (*ibid.* line 6) and "to pronounce the verdict of the wicked" ולחרוץ משפט רשעה (*ibid.* line 10). The judgment mentioned here is not routine jurisdiction in the court, because this usually takes place before the session of the רבים (6:1f.) (45). The main function of the council is to maintain "truth, righteousness and justice" within the community and "to keep truth in the land" לשמור אמונה בארץ (8:3) which is achieved by proper administration and management and not merely by judging a case in the court (46). This is true of every supreme council which represents a large community, as for example the Sanhedrin. Although the latter were involved in judgment of capital crimes, etc., their main activity was legislating and administrating on the national level, and they were considered the representative of the nation rather than a court. The author of the *Serekh* sees indeed in the council described in 1QS 8:1ff. the embodiment of truth in Israel (lines 5ff.). Through their just actions their community will become "an eternal plantation" מטעת עולם and "a holy house for Israel" בית קודש לישראל.

---

42 See F. de Cenival, *Les Associations Religieuses en Egypte, d'après les documents démotiques*, 1972, pp. 172-173.

43 The attempt to see in the fifteen men mentioned here a minimal cell of the community is forced (J. Licht, *Serakhim*, pp. 167ff.). As will be presently shown, the functions of this body are to supervise justice and maintain righteousness in the whole sect.

44 It is not impossible that the priests are included among the twelve, however, on the basis of comparison with 4Q 159 Ord (see below) it appears that the priests were in addition to the twelve.

45 No contradiction is to be seen therefore between 1QS 8:1f. and 1QS 6:1f. as has been argued by P. Wernberg-Møller, The Manual of Discipline, 1957, p. 122. Wernberg-Møller, tried to solve the difficulty by postulating different stages in the organization of the society but in the light of our explanation of the council in 1QS 8:1f. this is unnecessary.

46 The same applies to the concept of עשה משפט וצדקה in the Old Testament, for which see my book *Justice and Righteousness in Israel and the Nations in the light of Social Reforms in the Ancient Near East*, Jerusalem, 1985 (Hebrew)

A duodecimal court which consists of laymen and priests is found in the so-called 4Q Ordinances (47) where we read (48) about a court of twelve, including two priests, who are to be consulted on judicial matters : "ten men and two priests, and one shall be judged before these twelve... any capital case (דבר על נפש) (49); they will be inquired and whoever does not obey shall be put to death". This court bears a supreme character not only by its judging of capital cases but also by the injunction that whoever does not obey shall be put to death (compare Deut. 17:12).

A council on a national level comprised of twelve princes (נשיאי עם), twelve priests and twelve Levites is found in the Temple Scroll. These are "to sit at the side of the king for law and judgment (לתורה ולמשפט)... he will not do anything without taking counsel (עצה) from them" (50). In this capacity the council reminds us of the Sanhedrin (51).

A similar body, though in the cultic sphere, is described in the War Scroll :

... they shall appoint the heads of the priests twelve in number ... and after them there shall be the heads of the Levites, one for each tribe ... and the heads of the tribes ... subordinate to them and stationed constantly at the gates of the sanctuary (1QM 2:1-3).

A council of twelve priests and (twelve) heads of the tribes in an eschatological context is found in the *pesher* on Isa. 54:11-12 (52) : "... the twelve priests who give light by the judgment of the Urim and Thummim... the heads of the tribes of Israel..." (53). As has been shown by J. Baumgarten (54) the *pesher* refers to the judicial body of the ideal Jerusalem in the future. This body is reflected in the book of Revelation where the twelve apostles and the twelve angels of the tribes (ch. 21) constitute the tribunal of the twenty-four elders (ch. 4). Furthermore, according to Baumgarten the body of the twenty-three, the number of the *smaller Sanhedrin,* was also based on a quorum of twenty-four, the

---

47 *DJD* V, 1968, p. 8 (4Q Ord 159).
48 II:3-6.
49 דבר על נפש equals דיני נפשות in Rabbinic literature which means capital cases; for דבר in the sense of "case" (דין, משפט) see Ex. 18:16, 19, 22, Deut. 1:17; the same applies to Sumerian *inim*, Akkad. *awātum* and Hittite *memiyaš*, literally *word* but also meaning lawsuit, cf. M. Weinfeld, *Israel Oriental Studies* 7 (1977), p. 75. On the courts for capital crimes in the Second Temple period see E.E. Urbach, "Courts of Twenty Three", *Proceedings of the Fifth World Congress of Jewish Studies*, section 2, pp. 37ff. (Hebrew).
50 Col. 57, lines 11-13, Y. Yadin, *The Temple Scroll*, vol. II, 1977 (Hebrew).
51 Cf. Yadin, *ibid.*, vol I, 268ff. On the relation of the quorum of 36 to the 71 of the Sanhedrin see J. Baumgarten, "The Duodecimal Courts of Qumran, Revelation and the Sanhedrin", *JBL* 95 (1976), 59ff.
52 4Q 164, *DJD* V, pp. 27-28.
53 Cf. J. Baumgarten, *JBL* 95 (1976), 59ff. (see note 51) for a thorough analysis of the text.

number twenty-three resulting from the principle of avoiding an even-numbered court (compare Sanhedrin of seventy-one).

A council of twelve is also attested in the organization of the first Christian congregation in Jerusalem (Acts 1:13ff.) which seems to have represented 120 members (*ibid.* 1:15) (55). That the twelve apostles were considered a judicial body may be learned from Matt. 19:23, Luke 22:30 where it is mentioned that the apostles will sit on their thrones to judge the tribes of Israel.

Twelve as a representative body is also reflected in Targum Ps. Jonathan to Lev. 4:15. והקריבו הקהל פר בן בקר is rendered by : "and the twelve elders of the congregation which are appointed as counsellors (תריסר סבי כנישתא דמתמנן אמרכולין) will lay their hands on the head of the bull" (56). For a council of twelve for the management of a city compare שנים עשר טובי העיר in Tr. Soferim 19:8 (ed. Higer).

The institution of "twelve" did not begin with the Qumran sect (57). We find in Egypt important judicial courts from the Ramesside period comprised of twelve members (58). Similarly, according to Neh. 7:7 (cf. Ezra 2:1-2) the returnees from Babylon are lead by twelve persons (59).

Besides the number twelve we find also the numbers ten (60) and seven (61) as a quorum of a council, though these seem to have functioned in a lesser capacity than the twelve. This may be deduced from the fact that the twelve apostles, as the main council of the Christian community (Acts 1:13f. and see above) call an assembly ($\pi\lambda\tilde{\eta}\theta o\varsigma$) in order to nominate "the seven of good reputation" for taking care of the widow (Acts 6:1ff.). It also seems that the ten judges in CD 10:4f. (62) represent a smaller group than the other Qumran judiciary bodies of twelve mentioned above.

---

54 See previous note.
55 For 120 as a minimum necessary for creating a representative body cf. Mishnah Sanhedrin 1:6 : "And how many should there be in a city that it may be fit to have a Sanhedrin ? A hundred and twenty men".
56 On the nature of this council of twelve cf. A. Büchler, *Die Priester*, etc., p. 100.
57 *Pace* D. Flusser, *EI* 8 (1967), 52f.
58 See E. Seidl, *Einführung in die Aegypt. Rechtsgeschichte bis zum Ende des Neuen Reiches/3*, 1957, p. 32.
59 For the duodecimal system in the *thiasoi* in Palmyre, Dura-Europos and Petra cf. J.T. Milik, *Dédicaces Faites par des Dieux*, Recherches d'Epigraphie Proche-Orientale I, 1972, 119f.
60 Compare "ten elders" as a court in Ruth 4:6, "the ten rulers that are in the city" (Qoh. 7:19); cf. also Josephus *AJ* XX, 194 : δεκάπρωτοι. Judicial courts of ten members were customary in Egypt in the Ptolemaic period, see E. Seidl, *Ptolemäische Rechtsgeschichte*, 1962, pp. 69ff. Compare also the δεκάπρωτοι = Latin *decemprimi, decemviri* in the Greek-Roman municipalities.
61 Josephus, *Bel. Jud.* II, 570, *AJ* IV, 214, 287; compare שבעה משיבי טעם in Prov. 26:16 and שבעה טובי העיר in TB Megillah 26a, as well as the seven men of good reputation in Acts 6:3.
62 The judiciary body there consists of ten members, four of them priests and Levites.

The council of fifteen which stands at the head of the sect (1QS 8:1) and which was mentioned at the beginning of this section is also not an innovation of the Qumran sect. It is attested in the guilds and associations among the Labyads in Delphi (τοὶ πεντεκαίδεκα) (63) for example and others (64).

The presence of priests and Levites in the councils and courts mentioned above may be traced back to the Old Testament, cf. Deut. 17:9, 12, 19:17, Ezek. 44:24, 2 Chr. 19:5-11. According to the writings of the sect the priests were determinative in the council. This is said explicitly in 1QS 9:7 : "The sons of Aaron alone shall rule over judgment and property, according to them the decision shall be made" רק בני אהרן ימשלו הגורל (ו)יצא פיהם ועל ובהון במשפט (compare BS 45:17 : "and he made him (Aaron) rule over law and judgment" ומשפט בחוק וימשילהו). As will be seen below the priests held first place in the Qumran sessions and their meals.

III. The Priest, the Official (פקיד) and the Overseer (מבקר)

In the writings of the sect the priests hold first place in the organization : they sit in the first seats (1QS 6:8), they march first in the convenant ceremony (2:19-20), they are the first to bless over bread and wine (6:4-5) they have control over judgment and according to them the decision shall be made (9:7), and what is most important, according to their decision they accept or reject candidates into the sect. Next to the priest comes the פקיד בראש הרבים "the official at the head of the 'many'" who takes care of the organization of the sect and especially the admission of new members, etc. (1QS 6:14-15). After him comes the מבקר על מלאכת הרבים "the overseer over the possessions of the 'many'" who takes care of the economy and finances of the group (1QS 6:19-20).

A similar hierarchy is found in the cultic associations of the Hellenistic period. The ἱερεύς "priest", who in function equals the *magister* in the Roman associations (65), was considered the president of the guild. He of course presided over the cultic meetings of his group but he exerted no less influence in the more worldly matters of the association (66).

---

63 F. Solmsen, *Inscriptiones Graecae ad inlustrandas dialectos selectae* (4th edition by E. Fraenkel), 1930, 149; SEG 13, 366.18.203.
64 See Busolt-Swoboda, *Griechische Staatskunde*, pp.1299ff.
65 Cf. J.P. Waltzing, *Etude historique sur les corporations professionnelles chez les Romains* I, 1895, pp. 385ff.
66 M. San Nicolo, *Aegypt. Vereinswesen zur Zeit der Ptolemäer und Römer*, II, 1915, pp. 57ff.; F. Poland, *Vereinswesen*, pp. 339ff.

Next to him comes the ἐπιμελητής (= curator) (67) who was the administrative overseer of the group. Next in line comes the ταμίας (= quaestor) who was in charge of the economical-financial business of the group (68).

In the New Testament writings we find the ἐπίσκοπος (Acts 20:28, Phil. 1:1, 1 Tim. 3:2, Titus 1:7) as an overseeing officer —— a title which has been compared to the פקיד, מבקר of the writings of the sect, since both verbs, פקד and בקר were translated in LXX by ἐπισκοπεῖν. It is interesting to note that the מבקר is defined in the Covenant of Damascus as shepherding the flock and returning the lost (13,9), just as the ἐπίσκοποι are defined in Acts 20:28. These images apparently derive from the Biblical prophetic literature. Jeremiah speaks of the shepherds who scatter the sheep and do not watch (פקד) over them (23:1-2). Ezekiel, influenced by Jeremiah (69), speaks of tending (בקר) the sheep as a shepherd tends his flock (34:11-12). Thus, the two titles which we find in the Qumran sect writings, פקיד and מבקר have roots in Biblical literature, and the title "episkopos" (in the New Testament) is apparently their translation. Of note also is the fact that "episkopos" appears also in Hellenistic guilds (70), even if not so widely used.

In the cultic associations of Ptolemaic Egypt we find a similar hierarchy as well (71): The wr, "the great" is the priest responsible for sacral matters; mr šn is a kind of bursar and manager of the economy of the group and mr mš‘ is "in charge of the multitude" (see above) who was responsible for the social and administrative organization of the sect. The rwd, the president of the association, must also be mentioned here.

Regarding the roles of these functionaries, the rules of the Iobacchi (72) are illuminating. There we find the priest who deals with sacral matters and worship, and the ταμίας, responsible for properties and registration. The latter is authorized to appoint for himself a clerk γραμματεύς, should be find the need (lines 146ff.). From this we learn that the ταμίας was regularly able to fulfill also the function of γραμματεύς.

---

67 Josephus speaks of ἐπιμεληταί among the Essenes (*Bel. Jud.* II, 123, 129, 134).
68 Cf. the works of San Nicolo and Poland quoted in note 66. ταμίας translates in the Septuagint אשר על הבית "in charge of the palace" (Is. 22:15). המבקר על מלאכת הרבים "the inspector over the possessions of the Many" in 1QSa 6:19-20, indeed overlaps functionally the אשר על הבית in the royal economy of the First Temple period. According to Philo (*apud* Eusebius, *Praep. Evang.* VIII, II:10) the ταμίας among the Essenes was handling the salary and the economy of the community.
69 See Weinfeld, *ZAW* 88 (1967), pp.45ff.; see also Zech. 10:3, 11:16.
70 See e.g. Poland, *Vereinswesen*, pp. 377, 381.
71 See F. Cenival, *Les associations*, etc., pp. 153ff.
72 Dittenberger, *Sylloge/3*, no. 1109. For an analysis of the document see E. Drerup, "Ein antikes Vereinstatut", *Neue Jahrbücher für Klass. Altertum* III, 1899, pp. 356-370. For translation cf. below, pp.55-57.

A similar situation is found in the writings of the Qumran sect. Also here there is no absolute division of the above-mentioned functions, and it seems that the פקיד and the מבקר indicated at times the same person (73). Moreover, in the Damascus Covenant we hear that the מבקר directed the priest and teaches the "many" the teachings of the sect (13:9). Flexibility in these functions we find also in the cultic associations from Ptolemaic Egypt (74).

Among the Nabateans, in the memorial inscriptions to their sacerdotal leaders we find (75) a similar type of hierarchy : 1) the priest (כהנא or אפכלא (76)), 2) the "supervisor" מבקרא (77), 3) the scribe כתבא. Nabatean inscriptions reveal that the Nabateans fostered cultic associations, the so-called מרזח (78), for which see below.

IV. Acceptance of new members

In the matter of acceptance of a new member to the Sect there are important parallels in the Hellenistic cultic associations. Especially instructive on this issue is the code of the Iobacchi association from 178 C.E. (79). There we read : "No one shall become a Iobacchus unless he is first registered (ἀπογράψηται ... ἀπογραφήν) (80) in the usual manner with the priest and is approved (δοκιμασθῇ) by the vote (ψήφωι, casting lot) of the Iobacchi, εἰ ἄξιος φαίνοιτα καὶ ἐπιτήδειος τῷ βαχχειω — — as clearly being worthy and fit to be a member of the Bacchi. The entrance-fee shall be fifty denarii for one who is not the son of a member, while the sons of members shall register and pay ... half the usual subscription

---

73 See J. Licht, *Serakhim*, p. 115.
74 F. Cenival, *Les associations*, etc. pp. 163ff.
75 See A. Negev, "Nabatean Sanctuary at Jebel Moneijah", *IEJ* 27 (1977), 219-231.
76 A loanword from the Akkadian : *apkallu*. See S.A.Kaufman, *The Akkadian Influence on the Aramaic*, 1974, p. 34.
77 This term which was not clear in the Nabatean context (cf. A. Negev, *IEJ* 27 1977, p. 221 : "The interpretation of the title מבקרא ... is not at all certain") becomes now clear.
78 Cf. A. Negev, *IEJ* 13 (1963), 113ff.; J. Naveh, *IEJ* 17 (1967), 187f. See especially the inscription וחברוהי בני מרזח. On *mrzh* see recently J. Greenfield, "The Marzeah as a Social Institution", *Acta Antiqua* 22 (1974), 451-455.
79 Dittenberger, *Sylloge Inscript. Graec./3*, no. 1109 (see n. 72).
80 Literally : he will *lodge a written note*, but meaning : he will register. In our case the person who registers wants to join the group, all the members of which appear in the written record, compare 1 Esdras 8:30 : ἀπό γραφῆς (variants : ἀπογραφῆς) which translates Hebrew התיחש (Ezr. 8:3). For ἀπογραφῆς there and its comparison with LXX Ezr. 8:3, see R. Hanhart, *Text und Textgeschichte des I Esrabuches*, 1974, p. 81.

until the attainment of puberty ... When anyone has registered and has been approved by vote the priest shall give him a letter (stating) that he is a Iobacchus" (lines 32-62). The elements which we find here : registration, examination of the candidate and decision by vote are found in the Manual of Discipline and the Damascus Covenant :

The examination : In 1QS 6:14 we read that "the officer in charge of the many" (הפקיד בראש הרבים) shall inquire as to the mind (81) and deeds ot the candidate. In CD 13:11 the overseer (מבקר) is the one who examines the deeds and mind, etc., of all who join (82) the community. Elsewhere we hear that "mind and integrity" תום דרך, שכל (1QS 5:24) or "spirit and deeds" (רוח ומעשים) are examined. The first examination is done by the official (פקיד) or the overseer (מבקר) whereas the subsequent examinations are carried out by "the many" (הרבים). The latter ask the candidate "about his mind and his deeds according to the Torah" (1QS 6:18).

In the other Hellenistic associations we hear that the candidate is examined whether he is pure, pious and good (ἁγνός, εὐσεβεῖς καὶ ἀγαθός) (83). Similarly, in the Hippocratic oath the candidate swears (line 4) that he will keep his life and art in purity and holiness (ἁγνῶς καὶ ὁσίως) (84). In a medieval Hebrew paraphrase of the Hippocratic oath (85) we read that the Teacher should select a pupil suitable and virtuous in his behavior (הגון וטוב במעשיו).

The Registration in the סרך : Similar to the candidate of the Iobacchi community, who is registered and receives a certification (ἐπιστολή)

––––––

81 שכל here does not connote intellectual capacity but the ability to distinguish between good and evil and to acquire "knowledge of God". משכיל in Qumran literature (1QS 3:13, 9:12 etc.) as well as in Daniel (11:33, 35, 12:3, 10, compare 2 Chr. 30:22) should be understood in the religious sense and the same applies to דעת and יודע in Qumran literature (for דעת in Qumran W.D. Davies, *HThR* 46 (1953), pp. 113ff.). See F. Nötscher, *Zur theologischen Terminologie der Qumran Texte*, 1956, pp. 55-58; J.A. Sanders, *ZAW* 76 (1964), pp. 65ff.

82 נוסף here and in 1QS 6:14 (הוסף) is interchangeable with נאסף (cf. 1QS 5:7 : בהאספם ליחד), compare also in LXX προστιθέναι for (אל עמיו) נאסף. In later times of the Second Temple period the distinction between אסף and יסף was blurred completely. Thus 2 Kgs. 22:20 אספך על אבותיך ונאספת אל קברתיך בשלום is rendered by LXX προστίθημί σε πρὸς τοὺς πατέρας σου καὶ συναχθήσῃ εἰς τὸν τάφον σου whereas the same text in 2 Chr. 34:28 is rendered : καὶ προστίθημί σε πρὸς τοὺς πατέρας σου καὶ προστεθήσῃ πρὸς τὰ μνήματά σου. נאסף has the meaning of "enter" like late Hebrew נכנס (derived from כנס = אסף), cf. e.g., Deut. 22:2, Jud. 19:15. נוסף לעדה is to be understood therefore as נאסף = "enters".

83 Cf. E. Ziebarth, *Das Griechische Vereinswesen*, 1896, p. 141; F. Poland, *Vereinswesen*, p. 499.

84 Cf. W.H.S. Jones, *The Doctor's Oath*, 1924. Compare L. Edelstein, *The Hippocratic Oath*, 1943.

85 S.S. Kottek, J.O. Leibowitz, B. Richler, "A Hebrew Paraphrase of the Hippocratic Oath" (15th cent.Ms.), *Medical History* 22 (1978), pp. 438-445.

after passing the examination and being accepted, we hear in 1QS, and also in CD, that the candidate is registered after his acceptance in the order סרך according to his rank (1QS 5:23, 6:22 סרך תכונו) (86), though nothing is said about issuing a certificate to the new member.

The decision by lot : The volunteer (the candidate) "shall either draw near or stay away" (is accepted or rejected) according to the lot as comes forth from the council of Rabbim (1QS 6:16, 18-19, 22) and this is after he passes the examination (דרישה or פקידה). J. Licht, in his commentary to 1QS 5:3 connected the "lot" (גורל) in this context to the Greek ψῆφος, but doubted the possibility of Greek influence for this expression. Now, in the light of the parallel brought here which has voting by ψῆφος and also in view of the other parallels to the matter of accepting members into the communities, the possibility of influence appears more reasonable.

The oath : According to 1QS 5:8-10 every new member has to take an oath in public to keep the law of Moses. The oath at admission is also attested among the various Hellenistic guilds and associations (87).

Submitting private property : In the Hellenistic and Roman communities acceptance into the community is conditioned upon the payment of entrance dues (88). In the Qumran sect, which is based on joint-participation in property, the candidate transfers his property temporarily after the first year, and when the second year is completed, after he is accepted as a full-fledged member, he transfers his property completely (1QS 6: 18ff.) (89).

V. Law and Penalties

The penal code of the Qumran sect reveals a striking similarity to the codes of the various associations of the Greco-Roman period. Our discussion of this issue is divided into five sections :

---

86 Compare 1QS 7:21 : ונכתב בתכונו, 8:19 : יכתב בתכונו, CD 13:12 : וכתבוהו במקומו כפי היותו בגורל "and they shall register him in his place according to his lot". CD 14:4 : ויכתבו בשמותיהם איש אחר אחיהו "and they shall be enrolled by name each man after his brother". For the fixed order of the sessions in the Qumran community see below.
87 Cf. E. Ziebarth, *Das Griech. Vereinswesen*, pp. 141-142, see below p. 78.
88 Cf. F. Poland, *Geschichte des Griechischen Vereinswesen*, 1909, pp. 492ff.; M. San Nicolo, *Aegypt. Vereinswesen zur Zeit der Ptolem. und Römer* II, 1915, p. 27.
89 For a discussion of this problem see J. Licht, *Serakhim*, pp. 10ff.

1) violation of discipline and disturbance of order
2) ethics and morality
3) insulting sect members and leaders
4) laws of evidence
5) classes of penalties.

1) Violation of discipline and disturbance of order

a) *Infidelity :* As in the different sects of the Greco-Roman world
(90), the Qumran sect was also built on a voluntary basis. A person will-
fully joins the society and takes upon himself its code. If he betrays the
society, or infringes upon its code, his membership is cancelled. Should he
decide afterwards to return to the association he is considered a new candidate and must go through the same process as any new candidate would :

' The man whose spirit swerves from the congregation of the community, by dealing treacherously with the truth and by walking in the
stubbornness of his heart (91), if he comes back he shall be punished
two years : in the first he must not touch the pure thing of the Many... When two yars have elapsed, the Many shall be asked concerning
his affairs' (1QS 7:18-21, compare 6:13-23).

We read similarly in the Damascus Covenant :

' And the same is the case with every member of the congregation of
the men of perfect holiness who was loth to carry out the commands
of the upright men... When his deeds become apparent he shall be sent
away from the congregation like one whose lot has not fallen in the
midst of those 'taught of God' ... until the day when he shall again
stand in the conclave of the men of perfect holiness... (until then)
let no man agree with him in property and work for all the holy ones
of the Highmost have cursed him' (CD 20:2-8).

The possibility for return to the group after betrayal is given to a member
of relatively short seniority. A senior memeber who betrays is not given
the opportunity to return to the sect :

' And anybody who has been in the council of the community for as
long as a period of ten years, and whose spirit then backslides by
being treacherous towards the community, and he leaves the Many in
order to walk in the stubbornness of his heart (91), (such a one)
shall never come back to the council of the community' (1QS 7:22-24).

---

90 On the code of the association as a mutual agreement see M. San Nicolo, "Zur
Vereinsgerichtsbarkeit im Hellen. Aegypten", *Epitymbion*, pp. 296ff.
91 "Stubbornness of heart" (לב שרירות) here (compare 2:26, CD 8:19, 3:11-12)
and also in Deut. 29:18 expresses thought of rebellion, mainly in a context
of an aberration from the covenant. See M. Weinfeld, *Deuteronomy and the
Deuteronomic School*, 1972, pp. 195ff.

In the rules of the Pharisaic חבורה there is also the distinction between a senior member and a young member in the matter of return to the חבורה. A member who offends is severely dealt with upon his return (should he desire to repent), and according to Rabbi Meir "he is not accepted forever" (Tosephta Demai 2,9) (92) whereas the son of a member is dealt with leniently and permitted to be accepted as if he was a new member (93).

That seniority was obligating may be learned from the codes of the guilds in Ptolemaic Egypt. In Berlin Papyrus 3115 (94) we read that an embalmer (coachyt) must accept membership after spending ten years in the group. If after sixteen years he has not accepted membership, the other members will not eat or drink with him, and will not participate with him in the thirty-five days of mourning until he "takes his place" (95).

Of the obligation of a member to remain faithful to his sect we read clearly in the code of the guild of Zeus Hypsistos from Ptolemaic Egypt (69 to 58 B.C.E.) (96) : "And he shall not make factions (97) or leave the brotherhood (98) of the president (in order to pass) to another (group)".

A stipulation of similar nature is attested in the inscription of the Ein-Gedi synagogue formulated by the heads of the local professional guild (cultivating balsam) (99) where it says that the members shall not cause division between their fellows (יהב פלגו בן גבר לחבריה) and shall not reveal the secret of the town to the gentiles (גלי רזה דקרתה לעממיה) (100).

----

92 "And all those who have reverted are not accepted forever, the words of R. Meir", compare Abodah Zarah 7a, Bechoroth 31a. What is dealt with here are lay persons who reverted to their evil ways and now desire to receive membership anew; see Lieberman, *Tosefta Ki-fshutah*, order Zera'im, part I, p. 214.

93 "R. Shimon Ben Gamliel says : There is no similarity between a comrade who offends and the son of a comrade who offends" (*ibid.*, 2,14); see Lieberman (note 92), p. 217. On the distinction between a regular candidate and the son of a comrade in the matter of entrance into the community and membership dues, see the Iobacchi code (quoted above, p. 21; Dittenberger, *Sylloge/3*, 1109,37f.) and also in the Egyptian communities from the Ptolemaic period, W. Erichsen, *Die Satzungen einer ägyptischen Kultgenossenschaft aus der Ptolemäerzeit*, Pap. Prague 1959, lines 8-10; F. Cenival, *Les associations*, pp. 30-31 (discussion on *mnḫ*).

94 F. Cenival, *Les associations*, p. 15.

95 On the significance of "place" in the guilds see below.

96 Pap. London 2710, Recto 13-14, Roberts-Skeat-Nock, *HThR* 29 (1936), p. 40.

97 μηιὸὲ οχίματα ουνίοτασ[θαι], according to the editor (see preceding note) the correct reading should be : οχίοματα.

98 The Greek term for community here is φράτρα, the ancient Greek term for a religious association. The prohibiting of transferring from one group to another calls to mind the prohibition mentioned in regards to the Passover not to pass from one חבורה to another (TJ Pesahim 37d).

99 Cf. *Tarbiz* 40 (1970), pp. 18ff. and the discussions in the articles of B. Mazar, S. Lieberman and E.E. Urbach there (Hebrew), and see Appendix B.

b) *Disturbances in the assembly* : In the code of the Iobacchi (101) we read (lines 63-67) : "No one may either sing or create a disturbance (θορυβῆσαι) or clap his hands in a meeting but each shall say and act his allotted part with all good order and quietness under the direction of the priest...". In another place, next to a similar warning comes punishment (lines 107-110) : "No one shall deliver a speech without turning first to the priest... otherwise he shall pay thirty drachmas...".

In the Manual of Discipline :

' No one must speak in the middle of the speech of another member, (thus interrupting) before he has finished talking... At a session of the Many nobody must say anything which is not according to the pleasure of the Many... But any one who has something to say to the Many... that man may get on his feet and say : "I have something to say to the Many". If they say to him ("Speak"), then he may speak' (1QS 6:10-13).

And in regard to punishment : "For the one who interrupts his neighbor's speech (the fine is) ten days" (1QS 7:9-10).

In the Damascus Covenant :

' According to his word (the overseer's) shall the members of the congregation come, each man in his turn. And as for everything which any man has to speak to the overseer, let him speak with regard to any litigation and judgment' (CD 14:10).

Josephus relates of the Essenes : "No clamour or disturbance (θόρυ-βος) (102) ever pollutes their house (103); they speak in turn (ἐν τάξει) each making way for his neighbor" (BJ II, 132).

c) *Disturbances of the general order* : In the Manual of Discipline we find penalties for reclining and sleeping in the assembly of the "many", nudity, spitting inside the session of the "many", exposing of privates, loud laughter and baring parts of the body (1QS 7:10-15). Josephus also relates that the Essenes are careful not to spit in the midst of the group or to the right (BJ II, 147) (104).

We find no such detailing in other codes, but rather general instructions in this matter. In the Demotic code (Papyrus Lille 29) we read : "A man from among us who should cause disorder in the 'House' (com-

-----

100 For the text and its commentary see recently J. Naveh, *On Stone and Mosaic —— The Aramaic and Hebrew Inscriptions from Ancient Synagogues,* 1978, no. 70, pp. 105-109 (Hebrew); and see below p. 58.
101 Dittenberger, *Sylloge/3*, no. 1109, see Appendix A.
102 Compare θορυβῆσαι in the Iobacchi code mentioned above.
103 That is, "the sect". Compare the Aramaic Targums' translation of "house" by חבורה in Ex. 12:46.
104 Compare TJ Berachot 6d : "Even should he spit in order to clean his cup, it is forbidden in front of him but permitted behind him; it is forbidden to his right but permitted to his left".

munity)... let him have his punishment..." (105) and likewise in the Iobacchi code : "And should someone be found (behaving) out of order (εὑρεθῇ τις ἀκοσμῶν)... (106). In the Demotic papyrus from Tebtunis in the Fayyum we find a penalty for someone who should cause a disturbance after drinking wine (ἐκπαροινήσῃ) (107).

d) *Seating in fixed order* : In the session of the "Many" every man sits "according to his rank" (כתכונו) איש בתכונו, "the priests shall sit in the first seats, the elders in the next seats, and the rest of all the people shall sit, each in his definite seat" (1QS 6:4, 8-9). The members are registered "one before the other according to his mind and deeds" (*ibid.* 5:23).

A similar arrangement is established for the ideal community in the future :

' The priest shall come at the head of the whole congregation of Israel... Next shall come the Messiah of Israel and before him shall sit the heads of the thousands of Israel, each according to his rank... and all the heads of the fathers of the congregation... shall sit before them, each according to this rank (1QSa 2:11-17).

In the Damascus Covenant :

' And the order of the meeting of all camps. They shall be mustered all of them by names, the priests first, the Levites second, the children of Israel third and the proselyte fourth; and they shall be written down by name each man after his brother... And so they shall sit, and so they shall be asked about everything' (CD 14:4ff.).

The granting of permission to speak to members is determined according to the fixed sitting order in the community : "Nor must he speak before the definite rank of the one who is enlisted before him. The man, who is asked, may (only) speak in his turn" (1QS 6:10-11), which is said also in CD (11:14) and appears also in Josephus (BJ II, 132).

A similar procedure is found in connection with the session of the Sanhedrin (108). Students of the sages sit in three rows before the Sanhedrin, each one *knows his place* and does not change it as long as he is authorized for such (M. San. 4,4). Questions are also asked according to the hierarchy : "In cases concerning uncleanness and cleanness the judges declare their opinion beginning from the eldest" (*ibid.* 4,2). Like

––––––

105 Line 11, and see Cenival, *Les associations,* p. 5.
106 Dittenberger, *Sylloge/3,* no 1109, 73.
107 Pap. Michigan 243, 3 (Husselman, Boak, Edgerton, *Papyri from Tebtunis* II, 1944, p. 96).
108 See H. Rabin, *Qumran Studies,* 1957, pp. 104ff., who compares συνέδριον to מושב of the Qumran sect and to ישיבה in Rabbinic literature (see also Ben Sira 51:29 : בישיבתי).

the Sanhedrin, "the session of the 'Many'" (מושב הרבים) also met together for legal discussion and the members would be asked for advice on the issue (1QS 6:9, 7:21, 8:25-26).

A fixed sitting order is found also in the meals of the sect : "... and they shall eat together ... and each member shall sit according to his de- finite rank ... before him (= before the priest)" (1QS 6:4) and likewise in the meals in the hereafter :

'And if they are met for the common table ... let not any put forth his hand ... before the priest, for it is he who shall bless the first of the bread ... and next the Messiah of Israel shall put forth his hand on the bread. And then all the congregation of the community shall pronounce the blessing, each according to his rank' (1QSa 2:17-21).

Fixed seating arrangements are known from Rabbinic literature, both in communal meals and in the House of Study (*Beth HaMidrash*). So we find in the Tosephta exact סדרי הסב (reclining orders) and exactitude in the order of hand-washing and filling of cups :

'How is the order of reclining ? When there are two couches, the grea- ter reclines on the first one, the second to him beneath him. When there are three couches, the greater reclines on the middle one, the second to him above him, the third to him beneath him, and so forth.

How is the order of hand-washing ? Up to five they begin with the greater, from five and upwards they begin with the least.

How is the order of filling the cup ? During the meal, they begin with the greater. After the meal they begin with the one who makes the Benediction' (Tosephta, Berachoth 5,5-6).

Similarly, in the Rabbinic Academies (מתיבתא, ישיבה) we find rows of students who sit before the sages row within row and they would advance or demote according to the degree of learning of each student (109). The members of the "yeshivah" were called "the comrades" (חבריא) or "the brotherhood" (חברותא), since they would organize into small companies which maintained a communal life style which included group study and communal meals and living quarters (110).

Fixed seating arrangements were customary in guilds and associations in the Greco-Roman world. In the Iobacchi code we find a penalty for whoever takes the place of another member (111), and in the Tebtunis

---

109 See Baba Qama 117a; Megillah 28b; Hullin 137b.
110 See M. Beer, "The Emergence of the Talmudic Academy in Babylonia", *Pro- ceedings of the Fourth World Congress of Jewish Studies*, vol. I, 1967, pp. 99-101 (Hebrew).
111 *Sylloge/3*, 1109, 73 : ἐπ᾽ ἀλλοτρίαν ἐρχόμενος. The meaning of χλισία is a seat in the assembly for a session or a banquet.

Papyrus (112) we read that whoever takes the place of another member at a feast shall pay a fine in regards to his own place (τοῦ ἰδίου τόπου) (113). More closely parallel to our interest is the section in Papyrus London 2710, from the end of the Ptolemaic period. There we find a warning not to enter into another's pedigrees at the banquet (καὶ μὴι γενεαλογ[ήσειν] ἕτερος [τὸν] ἕτερον ἐν τῶι συμποσίῳ) (114). This calls to mind "each according to his honor" in the Manual of Discipline (1QSa 2:14, 17, 21).

In regards to the aforementioned documents it is difficult to determine when the occasion discussed is a banquet or a session, since in many cases the two were bound up together, as we find in ancient Mesopotamian literature (115) and in Greek literature (116). Ḥms, the Demotic "seat", which basically indicates assembly, is connected in the Demotic Codes with drinking (117), as in the London Greek papyrus 2710. The banquet (symposion) in the context of guilds is none other than a term for a group which organizes itself for libations, sacral meals, chanting of hymns and celebrating festivals (118).

e) *Absence from the assembly* : In the Manual of Discipline we read :
' ... and the same punishment applies to the man who goes away at a session of the Many, aimlessly and wantonly up to three times at a session, he shall be fined for ten days, but if they should hold a vote and he goes away, then he shall be fined for thirty days' (1QS 7: 10-12).

Ch. Rabin (119) is apparently right in his assertion that what is dealt with here is absence from place in the assembly for no reason. In my opinion, this absence consists in three exits (120) during one assembly which entails a light penalty : banishment for ten days. Ch. Rabin also correctly perceived that ואם יפקודו means "when they vote", that is, if he was absent at the time of a vote, his punishment is more grave —— banishment for thirty days. But contrary to Rabin's view יפקד does not

————

112 Husselman, Boak, Edgerton, *Papyri from Tebtunis* I, 1944, no. 243:6-7 (p. 96).
113 See in the Berlin Papyrus 3115, quoted above (p. 25) : "until he should take 'the place' (m3)", see also "placed" (m3.w) at a banquet in a Demotic ostracon which is a receipt for wine. See Cenival, *Les associations*, p. 182, n. 1. Compare also in Acts 1:25, and see below p. 48, section 5.
114 Lines 15-16 (*HThR* 29 (1963) p. 40), and see the explanation of Nock (above note 96), pp. 52-53. On the seating arrangements during a banquet see also Luke 14:7-11.
115 *Enuma eliš* III, 130ff. On the matter of the convocations of the gods as reflecting earthly assemblies see Th. Jacobsen, *JNES* 2 (1943), pp. 167ff., and especially note 49.
116 See e.g. *Iliad* II, 430ff.; Herodotus I, 133.
117 See Cenival, *Les associations*, p. 181.
118 Robert, Skeat, Nock, *HThR* 29 (1936), p. 85.
119 *Qumran Studies*, pp. 105ff.
120 On נפטר meaning "to go out" compare Mishna Yoma 1,5 : "took their leave (נפטרו) and went away...".

signify "stand" but rather "vote (by raising one's finger)". As הצביע is derived from אצבע (finger), so also (ה)זקף is derived from זקיפה which is also found meaning "finger" (B. Berachoth 45b, Pesahim 110a).

Penalties for non-participation in the assembly are found in the different codes of the various guilds (121), and the most severe penalty for non-appearance we find among the exiled community in the days of Ezra (122) :

' ... and that if anyone did not arrive within three days, it should be within the discretion of the chief officers and the elders to confiscate all his property and to exclude him from the community of the exiles' (Ezra 10:8).

2) Ethics and morality

The various communities in the Greco-Roman period maintained a high moral standard (123). The moral rules of these groups touch mainly on the mutual relationships within the framework of the community. But behind these rules is a recognizable general moral pathos. In the Qumran community code we find, as expected, moral precepts much more severe than in the pagan associations.

a) *Lying in relation to money and property* : In the Qumran sect which is based on joint-participation in property, the possibility arises for the embezzlement of public property. Therefore we find ordinances dealing with this matter which are not found in other associations :

' ... if there is a man among them who, though he knows, lies in a matter of property, they shall exclude him from the pure things of the Many for one year and he shall be fined one fourth of his food' (1QS 6:24-25).

' (...) with property, though he knows... (...) shall be punished for six days' (CD 14:20-21).

Apparently, not only the falsifier of the common property, but also of private property is dealt with. In another place in the Manual of Discipline we note that the sect members must pay damages from their own monies (1QS 7:6-8) which teaches us that besides the common assets of the community there existed also private resources (124).

---

121 Pap. London 2710:12 (*HThR* 29 (1936)); Pap. Michigan 244:7-9 (Huselman, Boak, Edgerton, *Papyri from Tebtunis* II); and compare M. San Nicolo, *Epitymbion*, 1927, pp. 270.
122 On the organization of the community of the exiles and its similarity to the organizations of sects in the days of the Second Temple, see my article in *VT* 23 (1973), pp. 72-75.
123 See F. Poland, *Gesch. d. griech. Vereinswesen*, pp. 499ff.
124 See J. Licht, *Serakhim*, on the text under discussion here.

An instructive analogy to this subject we find in the primitive Christian church in Jerusalem (125). In the Acts of the Apostles (5:1-11) is the account of Hannaniah and Shapira his wife who joined the early Christian community but both lied *knowingly* and held back from the price of the estate which they sold. For this they were punished and died. In the description of the act of lying we find a surprising similarity to the formulation of the Manual of Discipline and the Damascus Covenant. We read there in relation to this matter : "and he is aware (of it)" והוא ידע, which is comparable to συνειδυίης of Acts (compare ἢ σύνοιδεν in LXX Lev. 5:1 : "or knew" או ידע). In the Ptolemaic sects (126) the one who steals from the association or its Temple must pay a fine (127).

b) *Rules of modesty :* In the Greco-Roman societies we find statutes in matters of adultery (128), but we do not find statutes concerning modesty in general, as we find in the *Serekh* :

' The one who speaks with his mouth an improper word (shall be fined) for three months' (1QS 7:9) (129).

' Neither shall lewdness and iniquitious deceit be heard in my mouth, nor shall craftiness and lies be found on my lips. The fruit of holiness shall be on my tongue, and detested words shall not be found on it' (*ibid.* 10:21-23).

' He who shows himself in public insufficiently dressed... and the man who spits into the session of the Many... the one who stretches out his hand from under his cloak so that ... his nakedness is seen ... the one who guffaws improperly ... the one who stretches out his left hand ...' (*ibid.* 7:12ff.) (130).

c) *Mutual aid :* We hear of aid for the needy of the sect mainly from the Damascus Covenant :

' And this is the order of the Many for preparing all their requirements : The wages of two days in every month at least (131); and

---

125 See E. Haenchen, *The Acts of the Apostles,* 1971, pp. 236ff.
126 F. Cenival, *Les associations,* p. 5 (lines 9-10).
127 In Demotic : *ḳns.* For the explanation of the word see W. Erichsen, *Die Satzungen einer ägyptischen Kultgenossenschaft,* 1959, p. 30, though he was not aware of קנס in later Hebrew.
128 See M. San Nicolo, *Epitymbion,* pp. 276ff.
129 CD 10:18 : "And on the Sabbath day, let no man speak a lewd or villainous word", which is in proximity to "let him not speak of matters of labour and work to be done on the morrow" (line 19). Compare in the Rabbinic literature on Is. 58:13, and see R. Weiss, *Leshonenu* 37 (1973), p. 306 (Hebrew).
130 Compare above p.26 and the reference to Josephus there.

they shall place it in the hands of the overseer and the judges. From it they shall give for orphans and from it they shall strengthen the hand of the poor and the needy, and for the old man who dies, for the man who is homeless, for him who is taken prisoner by a foreign people, for the maiden that has no relative, and for the virgin who has no one to seek her (in marriage), all the work of the corporation...' (CD 14:12-16).

Thus we find here the giving of charity to the poor and orphans, aid in burying the dead and arranging his funeral, aid to the homeless (132), ransom of prisoners, and providing for the bride (133). Similarly, we read in the Damascus Covenant :

' To love each man his brother like himself; to strengthen the hand of the poor and the needy and stranger, to seek each man the well-being of his brother (134), not to sin each man against his kin of flesh' (CD 6:20ff.).

In the codes of the various sects, and especially in those from Egypt in the Greco-Roman period, we find many pericopes dealing with the issue of mutual aid (135). So for example we read there (136) that a person of the sect who should find his comrade in the harbor ($n3j(t)$) (137) with no means, and who gives him naught, shall pay a fine. The same holds for someone who is called to bury a member who died and did not come. Likewise, members of the community are obligated to participate in the mourning of a member in mourning, to participate in the funeral, to supply "mourner's bread" ('k nhpj) (138) and to drink with the mour-

––––––

131 That is, the minimal contribution is that of two days' wages, whereas there is no maximum limit. Compare Tosefta Peah 1,1 : "The Peah has a minimal extent, but no maximal extent", and see Hagigah 6b.

132 איש אשר ינוע means a person who is found outside of his home and is dependent on alms (cf. Ps. 59:16, 109:10); see L. Ginsberg, *An Unknown Jewish Sect*, 1976, p. 90, n. 314.

133 גמילות חסדים in Mishna Peah 1,1 implies such virtues. Compare Shabbat 127a and also Kiddushin 40a, and especially the form which crystallized in the frame of the Blessings of the sunrise in the Prayerbook, in which we find together with the providing of hospitality and the visiting of the sick also caring for the bride and attending funerals. On the text of the Prayerbook see A. Berliner, *Randbemerkungen zum täglichen Gebetbuch*, Berlin 1909. Compare also Ben Sira 7:33-34 and Matthew 25:31. On the matter of brotherly love as the foundation of the Essenes' sect see Philo *apud* Eusebius, *Praep. Evang.* VIII.11.2.

134 Compare "making peace between a man and his fellow" Mishna Peah 1,1.

135 Cenival, *Les associations*, pp. 193ff. Cf. also J.P. Waltzing, *Etudes Hist. sur les Corporations* I, pp. 314-315.

136 Pap. Lille 29, 15ff.; Pap. Cairo 30606, 13ff.; Pap. Cairo 31179, 13ff.; Pap. Cairo 30605, 12ff.; Pap. Prague 21ff.; Pap. Cairo 30619, 7ff. On all of these see F. Cenival, *Les associations*, pp. 193ff.

137 On this word see the analysis and discussion in Cenival, pp. 56-57. The meaning is that he chanced to be in a strange place and needs be given hospitality.

138 For the clarification of the concept see Erichsen, *Die Satzungen*, etc., p. 49 (mourner = nhpj). On "mourner's bread" see Hosea 9:4, and compare "They shall not break bread (see below) for a mourner to comfort him for a bereavement" in Jer. 16:7.

ner and raise his spirits (139). In these codes we also find sections dealing with the ransom of imprisoned members, and the obligation to give legal aid to members accused by the civil authorities.

We find similar statutes in Greek papyri from Egypt (140). Here we read (141) that if someone sees his comrade in strife ἐν ἀηδίᾳ (142) and does not help him, he shall pay a fine, and that the members of the community are obliged to release on probation a person who was arrested because of debt (143). Similarly we find here, as in the Demotic papyri, the obligation to participate in the mourning of a member in mourning (144), however, here we find in addition to the obligation to participate in the funeral and in the mourner's meal, also the obligation to shave the head, i.e., to make a bald patch ξυράσθωσαν (145) and to place a wreath on the grave withal (146).

The obligation to make a bald patch reminds us of the words of Jeremiah in relation to the house of mourning : "Great and small alike shall die in this land. They shall not be buried; men shall not lament them, nor gash and tonsure themselves for them" (16:16), which comes together with the mourner's meal and the cup of consolation in the context of accepted mourning customs. The prevention of the possibility to participate fully in the mourning of a bereaved person, according to the accepted custom, is interpreted by Jeremiah as the abrogation of peace, benefaction and mercy from the people : "... for I have withdrawn My favor from that people... My kindness and compassion," i.e., the desis-

---

139 Compare Jer. 16:7-8 : "They shall not break bread (read with the Septuagint ם‍ח‍ל) for a mourner to comfort his for a bereavement, nor offer one a cup of consolation for the loss of his father or mother. Nor shall you enter a house of feasting to sit down with them to eat and drink".

140 Husselman, Boak, Edgerton, *Papyri from Tebtunis* II, 1944, Pap. Michigan 243, 244.

141 Pap. Michigan 243, 6.

142 The editors translate "in trouble" (p. 99), but it may be that what is dealt with is a conflict and struggle, as found in the context of the Septuagint to Proverbs 23:19, and also in Aquila and Symacchus to Isaiah 41:12 and Jer. 15:10 (see Reider, *Index to Aquila*, *SVT* 12, p. 6). ἀηδία frequently accompanies nausea from drunkenness, see Liddell-Scott-Jones *s.v.*, and compare LXX to Proverbs 23:19.

143 Pap. Michigan 243, 8-9; 244, 9-10.

144 Pap. Michigan 243, 9-12; 244, 16-20.

145 ξυράω translates in LXX both the shaving of the head and the making of a bald patch.

146 Pap. Michigan 243, 9ff., and cp. in the code of the Iobacchi : "And if one of the Iobacchi should die they shall make for him a wreath in his honor... and one pitcher of wine shall be placed before each who takes part in the funeral, and whoever did not participate in the funeral shall not take part in the drinking of the wine" (*Sylloge*/3, 1109, 159ff.). In this code, therefore, there is no obligation to take part in the funeral, as found in the codes from Egypt. To be sure, the obligation of charitable deeds appears mostly in the codes of the eastern communities, whereas in the Greek communities it is very scarce, see Poland, *Gesch. d. Vereinswesen*, p. 502.

34

tance of philanthropic acts, and to be sure, the issue is interpreted thus in Tosephta Peah 4,21 :

' where do we find that charity and good works (גמלות חסדים) are a great peace and a *parakletos* beween Israel and their Father in heaven, as it is written, "Thus says the Lord, for I have withdrawn My favor from that people...My kindness and compassion (את החסד ואת הרחמים)". חסד means רחמים, גמילות חסדים means charity, hence charity and גמילות חסדים represent peace between Israel and their Father in heaven.'

d) *Applying to a court outside of the sect* : A member of the community takes upon himself the judgment of the community, and therefore it is forbidden him to apply to a court which is outside of the community. Already in the laws of Plato we find that if a dispute arises on the issue of membership dues to the association, it must be settled with the knowledge that no application to courts could be equitable in these cases (11, E 915). Accordingly, we find statutes on this issue in the Demotic papyri (147), in the Greek papyrus from Egypt (London 2710) (148) and in the code of the Iobacchi (149).

In the Qumran Sect we do not find an explicit statute on this matter of application to an external court (150), since it is self-understood. The sect does not recognize the legality of religious-legal institutions which are not of their chosen community. However, we find such a directive in the primitive Christian church. Paul enjoins the believers not to bring a legal case (πρᾶγμα) before the "unrighteous" (1 Corinthians 6:1) (151).

3) Insult of sect members and leaders
a) *Abuse of high ranking members and of the priest* : In 1QS 6:26ff. we read :

' And the one who answers his neighbor with a stiff neck and speaks with fury ... against the word of his neighbor who is enlisted before him, his hand has saved him (= he made justice for himself) (152)

147 Pap. Lille 29, 22; Pap. Cairo 30605, 19; Pap. Prague 17.
148 *HThR* 29 (1936), pp. 40-41, and there : μηιδὲ ἐπ[ικα]λήσειν καὶ μὴ κατηγορήσειν τοῦ ἑτέρου "Not to bring suit and not to accuse one another (before an external court)", and see the discussion there, pp. 53-54.
149 Dittenberger, *Sylloge/3*, 1109, 90-93 : "The same punishment shall be imposed on one who... fails to seek redress with the priest ... but has brought a charge before the public courts".
150 In Schechter's view (*Fragments of a Zadokite Work*) CD 9:1 implies a prohibition against being judged in the courts of the nations.
151 Cf. H. Conzelmann, *1 Corinthians, Hermeneia*, 1975, p. 104.
152 See CD 9:9-10. The Talmudic term for this is עשה דין לעצמו, cf. Baba Qamma 27b.

and shall be fined one year... But if it is against one of the priests...
that he speaks in wrath he shall be fined for one year and shall be put
into solitary confinement, excluded from the pure things of the Many'
(153).
The two instances treat of the abuse of a lesser to his greater —— the first
deals with disobedience to a higher ranking member, and the second with
abuse to a priest.

On abuse of the leadership and of the priests (154) we find pericope
in the Demotic codes such as Papyrus Cairo 30605 : "Anyone among us
who offends (hwš) (155) the 'commander of the many' (mr mšˁ) (156)
shall pay 50 shekels. And if he offends the secondary officer he shall pay
40. And if he offends on of the lay priests (= ˁšˀw) (157) he shall pay
60" (line 21) (158). Similar to the scroll of the Qumran sect, the Demotic
statutes open with the abuse of commanders and afterwards pass to abuse
of priests. Apparently "one of the priests who is written in the book
(הכתובים בספר)" in 1QS 7:2 means one of the lay priests, similar to
šˀw of the Demotic documents.

b) *Abuse of members of the sect* : In the Manual of Discipline we find
explicit statutes dealing with the abuse of members and slander against
them :
Provocation : "The one who gets angry at his comrade (159), shall be
fined for six months" (1QS 7:3-4).

———

153 In Licht's opinion (*Serakhim*) what is dealt with here is abuse which is not in
his presence, since it was already mentioned before that one who abuses his greater is banished for one year. However, it is possible that the lawmaker prescribes
an equal fine for one who rebels against the priest and for one who rebels against
his greater in rank.
154 On the priest as the leader of the Qumran sect see J. Licht, *Serakhim*, pp. 112ff.
(Hebrew).
155 The Greek equivalent to this verb is χαχολογεῖν (see F. Cenival, *Les associations*,
p. 30), or λοιδορεῖν (Sottas, *Papyrus demotiques de Lille*, 1921, p. 68, line 13),
and these words are indeed found in the various codes of the guilds, compare
Pap. London 2710 (*HThR* 29 (1936)), lines 15-16 : χαχολογ[ήσειν] : and also
the code of the Iobacchi, *Sylloge/3*, 1109, line 72 : λοιδορῶν.
156 See above, p. 20.
157 On šˀw as lay priests see the discussion in F. Cenival, *Les associations*, pp. 171ff.
158 F. Cenival, *Les associations*, pp. 77, and compare there Pap. 31179, line 24 and
30606, 19-20; see also Pap. Lille 29, 13 and Pap. Prague 14.
159 = ואשר יכעס (the interchange of ח/ע, like in עליפות instead of חליפות in 6:7);
במדעו = במודעו, that is, "his comrade" (cp. Prov. 7:4; Ruth 2:1).

Curse : "The man, who curses (160) wantonly at his neighbor (...) shall be fined for one year and shall be put into confinement" (*ibid.* 7:4-5). Arrogance and fraud : "The one who speaks to his neighbour with arrogance (see below) or plays false with his comrade, shall be fined for six months" (*ibid.* 7:5).

Gossip (slander) : "The man who walks round as a tale-bearer about his neighbor, they shall exclude him for one year from the pure things of the Many, and he shall be fined" (*ibid.* 7:15-16).

Comparable statutes, if not as fully detailed as these, we find in the codes of the guilds from the Greco-Roman period. In the Demotic statutes from the Ptolemaic period we find penalties for the one who offends (*hwš*) (161) his fellow member (162), and the fact that the size of the penalty is approximately half that of one who offends a priest (163) (*ꜥš3w*) (164) is instructive. The same relation exists in the statutes of the sect : the penalty of an abuser of a *comrade* is six months, as compared to the abuse of a *priest*, which entails a penalty of *one year*.

Other instances of abuse which are enumerated in the Demotic statutes are similar to those of the sect's. Thus we find there penalties for raising a hand against a member (165), for slander (*dj.t bjn*) (166), for ridicule or causing embarrassment to a member (*r. thth i.ir.ḥr.f*) (167) and for tale-bearing (*smj.r*) (168) before the authorities (169). A conspicuous difference in the statutes of the Qumran sect as against the Demotic statutes, is that in the sect's statutes there is no section on assault. This offense is much discussed in the statutes of the associations which we are dealing with here (170). We also find in the Demotic codes an especially severe penalty for one who ridicules his comrade by saying that he is a leper (171).

––––––

160 אצי in Syriac means "to curse" and indeed κακολογεῖν, which appears in the codes of the guilds (see n. 155) translates in the LXX קלל.
161 On the verb *hwš* see n. 155 above.
162 Pap. Cairo 30606, 19; 31179, 24; 20605, 20; Pap. Prague 14.
163 In Papyrus 30606, 25 deben for one who offends a fellow member and 40 for one who offends a priest; in Pap. 31179 : 50 deben for one who offends a member and 90 to one who offends a priest; in Pap. 30605 : 25 deben for one who offends a member and 60 for one who offends a priest.
164 See above, note 157.
165 Pap. Prague 11, 14, 15, and see Erichsen, *Die Satzungen*, p. 37.
166 Pap. Prague line 17, and the parallel places in the Demotic codes. For the explanation of the term see F. Cenival, *Les associations*, p. 54.
167 Pap. Prague, line 17, and see the discussion in Erichsen, *Die Satzungen*, p. 38.
168 On the distinction between *smj.r* and *dj.t bjn* see Cenival, *Les associations*, p. 54.
169 See Pap. Prague 17 and the parallels in Cenival, *Les associations*, p. 54.
170 See M. San Nicolo, "Vereinsgerichtsbarkeit", *Epitymbion*, p. 275.
171 Pap. Prague 19 and parallels. According to Pap. Cairo 30606, 18, the ridiculer must be banished from the community.

In the code of the Iobacchi (172) we read that one who instigates a quarrel, insults or slanders (ὑβρίζων ἢ λοιδορῶν) (173) is condemned according to two witnesses... and if someone should commit assault, the assaulted submits the indictment ... and the assaulter is temporarily banished from the community and pays a fine. The same penalty is prescribed for one who was assaulted and did not apply to the leaders of the community (the priest and similar authorities) but rather to a civilian court. It is interesting to note that the juxtaposition of the issues which we find in the code of the Iobacchi —— dispute and assault, insult, slander, informing to civilian authorities —— is the same juxtaposition found in the Demotic codes (174).

In a code from the days of Caesar Tiberius we read (175) :

'If a person should accuse his fellow, or inform on him (διαβολὴν ποιήσηται) (176) he shall be penalized eight drachmas. And if someone should devise a plot (ὑπονομένοη) (177) against his fellow or incites him (οἰκοφθορήοη) (178) he shall pay 60 drachmas.'

In London Papyrus 2710, from the guild of Zeus Hypsistos (69-58 B.C.E) we find that a member is forbidden to insult (curse, κακο-λογ[ήσειν]) (179) his fellow member in the community, and also to spread gossip (λαλήισειν), to sue or accuse (in an outside court).

The oath of the guild in En-Gedi quoted above (p. 25) should also be mentioned here, in which we find warnings against causing division between the members (דיהיב פלגו בן גבר לחבריה), slandering the members before the gentiles (אמר לשן ביש על חבריה לעממיה) and revealing the secret of the town (גלי רזה דקרתה לעממיא) (180).

----

172 *Sylloge*/3, 1109, 72ff.
173 ὑβρίζειν implies the meaning of "behave maliciously and with pride", and thus our section is parallel to the section in 1QS 7:5 : "The one who speaks to his neighbour with arrogance". There is therefore no need to explain מרום as from רמיה, as is usually done (see Wernberg-Møller and Licht in their commentaries), but rather from רום; cp. Ps. 73:8 : they speak arrogantly (ממרום) which comes in a context of speaking evil : "They scoff and plan evil; ... They set their mouths in heaven, and their tongues range over the earth". On λοιδορεῖν see above, n. 155.
174 See Pap. Prague, line 14ff. and the parallels in the Cairo papyri : 30606, 17f.; 31179, 20f.: 30605, 21f.
175 Husselman, Boak, Edgerton, Michigan *Papyri from Tebtunis* II, 1944, no. 243, 7f.
176 διαβάλλειν in LXX to Daniel 3:8 (also in Theodotion) translates אכל קרץ "to inform".
177 Cp. ὑπονοθεύειν in II Macc. 4:26 in connection with the plots of Jason.
178 The verb appears frequently in a context of seduction see Liddell-Scott-Jones *s.v.*
179 Roberts-Skeat-Nock, *HThR* 29 (1936), lines 15f.
180 See note 100; and pp. 61-62 below.

Matthew 5:22 is also relevant to this issue : "Anyone who nurses anger against his brother (some witnesses insert 'without good cause') must be brought to judgment. If he abuses his brother he must answer for it to the court; if he sneers at him he will have to answer for it in the fires of hell" (181).

c) *Abuse of members' or sect's property* :

' ... but if it is against his neighbor that he commits a fraud, he shall be fined for three months, and if it is with the property of the community that he behaves fraudulently, and he cannot afford to refund it, he shall be fined for sixty days' (1QS 7:6-8).

Similar sections are to be found in the codes of the various guilds. Thus, for example, in the Demotic Papyrus Lille 29, where we find before the sections dealing with abuse and insult : "And if one from among us should steal money, property or any other thing from the inner house (ẖn), if the matter be proven ... he shall pay..." (182). Similarly, in the oath of the local guild in En-Gedi there is a clause against stealing property of the members (גניב צבותיה דחבריה) (183).

4) Laws of evidence

a) *Witnesses and proof* : In the Qumran sect there is exacting rigor as regards a fair trial for members who trespassed. The guilt of a member must be proven by witnesses, and if someone should act as a false witness, he is punished.

Thus we read in the Manual of Discipline :

' ... nor must anyone bring up any case (184) against his neighbor before the Many without proof before witnesses' (1QS 6:1).

' ... but if it is against his neighbor that he grumbles wantonly, then he shall be fined for six months' (*ibid.* 7:17-18).

And similarly in the Damascus Covenant :

' ... every man of the members of the covenant who brings against his neighbor an accusation (184) without proving before witnesses... he is one who takes vengeance and bears rancour...' (185) (CD 9:2-4).

Comparable to these prescriptions we find in the Demotic Papyrus Lille 29, on the matter of trespasses : "If the issue be proved against him

---

181 In connection with the last sentence compare Baba Mezia 58b : "All who descend into Gehenna (subsequently) reascend, excepting three ... ho who publicly shames his neighbor, or fastens an evil epithet upon his neighbor".
182 Cenival, *Les associations*, p. 5, lines 9-10.
183 See below p. 58.
184 For דבר as "dispute", compare Ex. 18:19, 22, and see my article in *Israel Oriental Studies* 7 (1977), p. 69, n. 20, p. 75, n. 65. The same meaning is found also for Akkadian *awātum*, Sumerian *inim* and Hittite *memiyaš*.
185 That is, transgresses the comandment "You shall not take vengeance or bear a grudge against your kinfolk" (Lev. 19:18); see below p. 40f.

(*iw.s 'ḥ'r rd.wj n.f*) (186) (or "for him") (187). Another parallel is found in the Iobacchi code (188) :

' And if someone should start a dispute or be found out of order, usurping the place of another or insulting or slandering (ὑβρίζων ἢ λοιδορῶν), the insulted and the slandered person shall bring two witnesses of the Iobacchi who have been forsworn (ἐνόρχιοι δύο...) (189) that they heard him insulting and slandering, and the insulter and slanderer shall pay the community twenty-five drachmas, or the person who caused the dispute shall pay the same sum...

And if anyone come to blows, he who has been struck shall lodge a written statement (190) with the priest... and he shall without fail convene a general meeting, and the Iobacchi shall decide the question by vote... and the penalty shall be exclusion for a period to be determined and a fine not exceeding twenty-five silver denarii. And the same punishment shall be imposed also on one who, having been struck, fails to seek redress with the priest... but has brought a charge before the public courts' (191).

We find here also, as in the Qumran sect, that the accuser must bring witnesses; and if it becomes clear that the accuser caused dissension, he will also be suitably punished.

A similar procedure to that of the Iobacchi code is reflected also in Matthew 18:15ff :

' If your brother commits a sin (some witnesses insert 'against you'), go and take the matter up with him (ἔλεγξον αὐτόν), strictly between yourselves... If he will not listen, take one or two others with you, so that all facts may be duly established on the evidence of two or three witnesses. If he refuses to listen to them, report the matter to the congregation (ἐκκλησία); and if he will not listen even to the congregation, you must then treat him as you would a pagan or a tax-gatherer.'

As in the Iobacchi code, also here we find two stages in the trial, according to the gravity of the deed : 1) two witnesses and the judge; 2) a trial

---

186 Literally, "if the dispute stands on its feet against him'" a concept which is comparable to Greek ἐπίδειξις. See Sethe-Partsch, *Demotische Urkunden zum ägyptischen Bürgschaftsrecht*, pp. 194ff., sect. 74e; p. 279, sect. 45.
187 Lines 9, 13, 14, 15, 19, 22, 25 (F. Cenival, *Les associations*, pp. 5ff.).
188 *Sylloge/3*, 1109, 72f., and cp. above p.37.
189 On the swearing of witnesses in Greece, before their giving testimony, see J.H. Lipsius, *Das attische Recht* II, 1915, pp. 884f.
190 On the written indictment see the discussion in M. San Nicolo, "Vereinsgerichtsbarkeit", *Epitymbion*, p. 290, n. 140.
191 Compare also the code of the Labyads, *Sylloge* II/2, 438:125f. and also IG/2, 1275, cited in San Nicolo (preceding note) p. 290.

in the presence of the whole congregation. Apparently, the last sentence above, is meant to say that if the accused will not listen to the assembly, it is possible to relate to him as if he were expelled from the community and therefore permissable to bring him before the civil courts.

b) *Reproof of a member in sincerity and on the same day* : As in other issues, this issue also deviates from legal, formalistic wording and passes into moral sermonizing. Before a member brings his accusation before the judicial body, he should reprove the member at fault in sincerity, humility and in love :

'They shall admonish one another in truth, humility, and affectionate love. He must not speak to him with anger or with a snarl, or with a stiff neck... in a spirit of ungodliness, and he must not hate him... of his heart, for he shall admonish him at once, so that he does not bear sin because of him (1QS 5:24-6:1).

Only after this passage comes the section which says : "... nor must anyone bring up any case against his neighbor before the Many without proof before witnesses", quoted above.

Similarly, in the Damascus Covenant we read : "... to reprove each man his brother according to the comandment and not to bear rancour from one day to the next" (CD 7:2). And also *ibid.* 9:6-8 :

'if he kept silent at him from one day to the next, and spoke about him when he got angry with him, it was a capital matter that he testified against him (192), because he did not carry out the commandment of God, who said to him : "Thou shalt surely reprove thy neighbor and not bear sin because of him".'

Very close to these demands is the demand of Hebrews 3:12-15 :

'See to it, brothers, that no one among you has the wicked, faithless heart of a deserter from the living God; but day by day, while that word "Today" still sounds in your ears, exhort (παραχαλεῖτε) (193) one another, so that no one of you is made stubborn by the wiles of sin. As Scripture says, "Today if you hear his voice, do not grow stubborn as in those days of rebellion...".

In all the above-mentioned sources there is a demand to reprove the accused person on the same day, and it seems that the issue referred to is a sectarian homiletic interpretation of scripture (194). The passage from

————

192 For the various suggestions for the interpretation of this sentence see Ch. Rabin, *Zadokite Documents, ad loc.*
193 According to the context the verb παραχαλεῖν here should be understood as "to warn and reprove"; see the Hebrew translation of F. Delitzsch, and cf. also 2 Corinthians 10:1.
194 The midrash is based on Numbers 30, where a husband is enjoined to respond to the vows of his wife or daughter on the same day (verses 6, 8, 9, 13, 15); in CD 9:6 the verse from Num. 30:15 is quoted in proximity to Lev 19:17.

Matthew 18:15ff. (195) belongs also to this issue, and this is the case in Ben-Sira 19:12ff. as well (see also the discussion below pp.74-75).

5) Classes of penalties

A pecuniary fine is among the most customary penalties in Ptolemaic and Hellenistic communities (196). Clearly, this penalty is out of place in the Qumran sect, which is based on joint capital. Only once do we find the payment of a fine in the Qumran sect —— when a member causes damage to the common property of the sect : "... and if it is with the property of the community that he behaves fraudulently, and he wastes it, then he shall refund it in full (...) If he cannot afford to refund it, he shall be fined for sixty days" (1QS 7:6-8). It is difficult to give a reasonable explanation for this exception (197). The problem is especially difficult since the clause is fragmented in the middle. Apparently, we have here a penalty of *lex talionis* : He who damages property must pay his penalty in property; Rabin (197a) rightly suggested that the use of property in the sect was communal but the owners retained the actual ownership. A member could use then his property to pay fines.

The most customary punishment in the Qumran sect is the ostracism of a member from the community, whether the time of banishment is limited or permanent. This penalty is known to us also from the Egyptian and Hellenistic associations. Comparable to what is found concerning the Qumran sect members (see below) in these associations too the meaning of banishment is : deprivation of participation in the worship of the community, prevention from holding office and denial of certain rights (198); however, the payment of fines is the decisive penalty in these communities. We frequently find both the payment of a fine and ostracism temporary or permanent (199).

a) *Absolute expulsion* : According to the statutes of the Qumran community, absolute banishment is proscribed for the following cases : 1) intentional violation of the law of Moses (1QS 8:22-24); 2) using the name of God (tetragram) in vain (*ibid.* 6:26-7:2); 3) slandering the sect

_____

195 "But if thy brother sin against thee, go, reprove him between thee and him alone", and compare Maimonides, הלכות דעות, 6, 7 : "He who reproves his fellow ... must reprove him between him and himself".
196 See M. San Nicolo, "Vereinsgerichtsbarkeit", *Epitymbion*, pp. 281ff.
197 See J. Licht, *Serakhim*, pp. 10-12 (section 11), in connection with the various possibilities for solving the difficulty.
197a Rabin, *Qumran Studies*, 1957, pp. 22-31.
198 See M. San Nicolo, *Aegypt. Vereinswesen* II, pp. 194ff.
199 In the Demotic documents this double punishment is found for the adulterer and for the one who ridicules his fellow by calling him a leper, Pap. Lille 29, 25; Pap. Cairo 30606, 18; Pap. Cairo 31179, 22. In Pap. Prague line 19 both punishments are said only for the adulterer. On banishment and fine together in the Hellenistic communities see IG II/2 1361, 13ff.; IG XII, 3, 330:263f. : στερέσθω τοῦ κοινοῦ καὶ ὀφειλέτω αὐτῶι δραχμὰς πεντακοσίας.

(*ibid.* 7:16-17); 4) non-acceptance of the sect's authority (*ibid.* 7:17); 5) betrayal of the sect (*ibid.* 7:22-25).

In the Demotic codes, this penalty is proscribed for adultery and for one who slanders a member that is a leper (see note 199). In the code of the Qumran sect the adulterer is included among those who trespass the law of Moses, and therefore, there is no need for special mention (200). Similarly, it is important to remember that the Qumran sect was basically a men's society (at least in the sect as it is reflected in the ordinances), thus, a special warning against adultery is out of place. As regards the grave penalty in the Demotic code for one who slanders a fellow member by saying he is a leper, apparently this is a matter of *lex talionis* : the leper can expect to be expelled from the society (201), and therefore that which the slanderer plots to do, shall be done to him.

Treason and rebellion comprise most natural reasons for banishment and seclusion from the sect, especially when the issue is one of a person who entered the sect out of his own free will. Non-acceptance of the group's authority serves as ground for ostracism in the Hellenistic communities as well (202).

On the expulsion from the Pharisaic חבורה we hear in Tosephta Demai 3,4 and also in B. Bechoroth 31a and J.Bechoroth 2,3, fol. 23a. The expression in these passages is : "they expel him from his group" (דוחין אותו מחבורתו). As we saw above (203) in the code of the Qumran sect, in the Pharisaic law as well, persons "who retracted" (חזרו בהן) from the sect, that is to say, who were full members and withdrew, are permanently expelled. The "sons of the members" (בני חבר), i.e. not full members (204) are received even after they have withdrawn.

b) *Temporary expulsion* : Temporary expulsion ranges from a period of ten days to a period of two years, depending on the gravity of the trespass (205). Gradation of penalty is found in the Demotic codes, however there the gradation concerns monetary fines (206). Significantly, there is no agreement between the various communities concerning the relation of the gravity of offense and the fine imposed on its execution (except regarding the most serious offenses) (207). This can be

---

200 An allusion may be found in CD 7:1-2; 8:5; Compare 1 Cor. chap.5. .
201 In Egypt also, as in Israel (Lev. 13:46, Num. 5:1, 2 Kgs. 7:3), lepers were put off from the community or from the settlement (cp. *Against Apion* I, 26, 31ff., and see the comments of F. Cenival, *Les associations*, pp. 28-29).
202 M. San Nicolo, "Vereinsgerichtsbarkeit", *Epitymbion*, pp. 279-280, and the literature there.
203 Above, pp.24.
204 Above, pp. 25.
205 See the discussion of J. Licht, *Serakhim*, pp. 155ff.
206 See the table in F. Cenival, *Les associations*, pp. 200-210.
207 See above, p.41.

explained by the fact that every society is autonomous and decides on penalties with the assent of its members and in accordance with the special conditions of each community. Therefore, there is also no place for compromises, or for leaving the matter of decision on the extent of penalty in the hands of judges. The judges only determine whether a crime was actually committed, and it is not in their capacity to be lenient or stringent. Every member takes upon himself, at the time of his entrance into the community, the ordinances regarding penalties fixed by the Assembly and thus he is aware of what is in store for him however he should act. The code thus bears the character of an immutable agreement (208).

c) *Exclusion from communal activity* : A member who was expelled cannot use the communal property, is considered apart from the purity of the "Many", and is also banished from the seat of advice and judgment (1QS 8:22ff; compare 7:17ff.). The separation from purity means the setting apart from the communal meal. This penalty we find in the Berlin papyrus 3115 (209) : "A man who passes 16 years without joining the association of Amen-Opet, not one of the men of the 'house' shall eat or drink with him". We find similar penalties in the Greco-Roman guilds (210).

VI. Period of probation for a candidate

A candidate for membership in the sect passes a period of trial of two years (1QS 6:21). After this period the candidate takes part in a swearing-in ceremony and is accepted as a full member of the sect (*ibid.* 5:8, 20) (211). We hear of a period of trial also in the various Greco-Roman associations (212). In certain of these the candidates are called "silent ones" (213). It seems to me that these "silent" candidates appear

208 See M. San Nicolo, "Vereinsgerichtsbarkeit", *Epitymbion,* p. 298.
209 F. Cenival, *Les associations,* p. 103, line 3.
210 M. San Nicolo, "Vereinsgerichtsbarkeit", *Epitymbion,* p. 280, n. 113.
211 Compare Josephus, *Bel. Jud.* II, 137-139. In the view of H. Hakkak (*Shnaton* 1, pp. 155ff.) col. 5 of the Manual of Discipline reflects the final ceremony, and the account of Josephus supports his assumption. For two stages of candidature see P. V. Osten-Sacken, *ZNW* 55 (1964), pp. 19-20.
212 See the discussion in H. Ch. Youtie, "The Kline of Sarapis", *HThR* 41 (1948), pp. 20ff.
213 In an inscription from Rome from the 2nd century C.E. we find a list of 400 members of the Bacchanalian association, ordered according to the rank of the members, cf. F. Cumont, "La grande inscription bacchique", *American Journal of Archaeology* 37 (1933), p. 232. At the end of the list appears the word σιγηταί (23) "the silent ones" in the meaning of "the candidates", who do not have the right to speak or vote, see Youtie, *HThR* 41 (1948), pp. 20-21.

in 1QS 7:20. There it is said that the candidate for membership (in this case, after he was punished) is not to partake of the banquet of the "Many" during his second year "and he shall sit behind all the (other) men of the community". This sentence instructs us that the candidates who sat behind the community are members without the right to participate in discussion (214) and to be sure, immediately after this is mentioned that "when two years have elapsed the Many shall be asked concerning his affairs. If they admit him, *he shall be asked concerning judgment*" (1QS 7:21).

A longer period of trial is to be found in the Demotic code, Berlin papyrus 3115 (215) :

' Any man who spends ten years with the embalmers (coachytes) must take upon himself membership. Every one (of the embalmers) who passes 16 years without joining the society of Amen-Opet, not one of the men of the "house" shall eat or drink with him' (lines 2-3) (216).

From Hippolytus (see below p. 70) we hear of a period of trial for candidates of the early Christian congregations. The candidates undergo a period of three years' preparation before they are accepted as members. Similar to what we found in 1QS, these candidates also undergo tests twice : when they join the association and at the end of the period of candidacy (217). As in the Manual of discipline (see above p.22) so also according to the Apostolic tradition of Hippolytus the candidates are tested as to their qualities, deeds and character (see p. 70).

VII. Renewal of validity of the code

The codes of the Egyptian guilds are valid for one year (218), and so we find in the scrolls of the Qumran sect that the covenant is renewed every year : "Thus they shall do year after year" (1QS 2:19; compare 5:24). The custom of the yearly renewal of covenants and obligations

---

214 See Licht, *Serakhim,* on this passage.
215 F. Cenival, *Les associations,* p. 103.
216 It is possible that the prohibition forbidding the man of God from Judah to eat and drink in Beth El (1 Kgs. 13:8ff.) originates in a *tabu* cast upon Beth El and its prophets by the guild of prophets of Judah.
217 See the discussion and references in I.F. Baer, *Zion* 29 (1964), p. 35, n. 95 (Hebrew).
218 F. Cenival, *Les associations,* pp. 146-147.

is an ancient one (219). We find an Egyptian code from the Persian period in which it is declared that its validity is for one year (220). The need for yearly renewal of the covenant does not testify as to the impotency of its validity, rather it instructs us on the importance of the obligation which must be reiterated and inrooted in the consciousness by means of yearly ceremony and assembly (221).

VIII. The Founder of the Sect

In the associations from the Greco-Roman period a special importance is attributed to the founder of the community, κτίστης (222). In many instances the community arose only after the death of the founder, on the authority of his words and testament. It occurs that the community is named after the founder (223). Apparently, the "Teacher of Righteousness" of the Damascus Scroll is to be considered as κτίστης. In the beginning of this scroll, in the section bearing the character of a historical introduction, we read that the men of the Sect were as blind men and seekers of the way for twenty years, and then God rose up for them "a Teacher of Righteousness to lead them in the way of His heart" (CD 1:9ff.). The "Teacher of Righteousness" was a priest, as can be learned from the Commentary of Psalm 37 which speaks of a priest, teacher of righteousness, as the founder of the sect : "Its interpretation concerns the Priest, the Teacher of Righteousness whom God commanded to arise (224) and (whom) he established to build for him a congregation..." (225). As we already mentioned, the priest held first place also in the Hellenistic associations (above p. 19) and it is only natural that the founder of the religious community should be a priest as well.

———

219 See my article "The Loyalty Oath", *UF* 8 (1976), pp. 393-394 and also VT 23 23 (1973), p. 72, n. 1.
220 The fragmented text opens with the words : "Twelve months which are one year", and after this come the ordinances regarding the obligation to appear at funerals (387 B.C.E.). See Roberts, Skeat, Nock, *HThR* 29 (1937), pp. 84-85; F. Cenival, *Les associations*, p. 213, n. 3.
221 See on this issue E. Seidl, *Ptolemäische Rechtsgeschichte* 1962, p. 154.
222 F. Poland, *Gesch. d. griech. Vereinswesens*, pp. 272ff.; M. San Nicolo, *Aegypt. Vereinswesen* II, p. 7ff.
223 See the references in San Nicolo, preceding note.
224 לעמוד instead of לקום, compare the passage from the Damascus Covenant mentioned above : ויקם להם מורה צדק (1:11). On the use of עמד in later linguistic layers, as opposed to קום in the earlier period see A. Hurvitz, *The Transition Period in Biblical Hebrew*, Jerusalem, 1972, p. 173 (Hebrew).
225 *DJD* V, Qumran cave 4, p. 44, III:15f.

IX. The differences between the codes of pagan guilds and the code of the Qumran Sect

Even though from the aspect of the legal issues and appellations of the sect we find an overlapping between the Qumran Sect and the various associations from the Greco-Roman period, from the aspect of the content of their codes there exist conspicuous differences between them. We shall indicate the most prominent among them :

1) In the various associations we find ordinances concerning sacrifice and oblations and convocations in temples on holidays (226), a matter which is completely absent from scrolls of the Sect. This situation can be understood in view of the fact that the sect members were cut off from the Temple in Jerusalem.

2) Ordinances in regards to funeral and burial, and rites such as the mourner's meal etc., which were widely dispersed in the codes of the associations (227) and which were an important factor in the crystallization of the various associations (228), are absent from the ordinances of the Sect. It is possible that this absence derives from the reservations towards "funerary sacrifices" (זבחי מתים), a demurrer which typified the Jewish religion in general. However, it seems that in a sect whose members live within a common framework, in the same place, there is no need to propound and encourage participation in mourning rites and their like. The normal rite was observed without difficulty since all the members were present in place and did not venture far one from another.

3) Ordinances concerning the payment of membership dues and pecuniary fines, which take up the major portion of the codes of guilds and associations are entirely out of place in a sect based on joint-participation in property.

As against the elements mentioned above, which we do not find in the Qumran Sect, we find in the Sect's code many elements which are uninstanced in the pagan associations :

4) The entering into the covenant which is accompanied by a blessing and a curse, found in the Qumran community (1QS 1:16-2:25) is unparalleled in the codes of the various communities. Apparently, in this

226 F. Cenival, *Les associations*, pp. 177ff.
227 *Ibid.*, pp. 187ff., and on the Greek and Roman associations see F. Poland, *Gesch. d. griech. Vereinswesen*, pp. 503ff.
228 מרזח which is the most ancient term for a cultic association prevailing from Ugarit of the 14th cent. B.C.E. to Palmyra of the 3rd cent. C.E., was mainly dedicated to funerary rites associated with the meals after burial (Cf. Jer. 16: 5 and see above).

matter the Sect continues an ancient Israelite tradition of covenant ceremonies (229).

5) The religious-moralistic rhetoric which adjoins the ordinances of the
Sect is not to be found in the ordinances of pagan associations. This ele-
ment is especially prominent not only in regards to the codes of the pagan
associations, but also in regards to the laws of Israel in general. In contrast
to the law codes of the Ancient Near East which lack motivation, rhetoric and argument, Israelite law (230) abounds in sermonizing and appeal
to the emotions.

6) Closely related in their character to the above difference are the instances of hymn and praise which we find in the Manual of Discipline
(10:9ff.) which are connected apparently with the prayers and hymns of
the sect members. It is possible that the presence of these intrusions of
song/poetry in the code of the Sect originate in the peculiar religious
fervor which the Judean Desert Sect exhibits.

7) The Qumran sect formulated its code not only for the present but
also for the ideal future, that is, "The Rule of the Community in the
hereafter". Since the sect members were cut off from the community of
Israel which was unified around the Temple in Jerusalem, a deep longing
was implanted in them for the renewal of the ideal community in the future. Out of this longing developed the practical statutes for the formation
of this community when it should be established in the future.

---

229 See J. Licht, *Serakhim*, pp. 53ff., and also H. Hakkak, *Shnaton* 1, pp. 155ff.
The view of J.F. Baer, *Zion* 29 (1964), pp. 4ff. (Hebrew), that the rite and the
confession in the Manual of Discipline originate in the Christian ceremonies for
the κατηχούμενος is unfounded. A rite accompanying a confession is found in
connection with the covenant of Nehemiah (Neh. 8-10). Fundamentally, the rite
in Nehemiah is no different from the rite of initiation into the covenant in the
Manual of Discipline. The Christian congregations actually continued with the
initiation ceremonies as observed in the Jewish community. It goes without saying
that the parallels which we bring for the customs of the sect from the Ptolemaic
communities completely refute the assumption of Baer as to the Christian origin
of the Qumran Sect.
230 We refer mainly to the priestly and Deuteronomistic law, as opposed to the law
of the Book of the Covenant. In the laws peculiar to Israel found in this ancient
corpus, it is possible to reveal also a bit of rhetoricism (Ex. 22:20ff.), but not to
the same extent as that found in P or D. On the oratory in Deuteronomy see
M. Weinfeld, *Deuteronomy*, etc., pp. 282ff.

X. The primitive Christian community and the
sectarian organizational patterns

In our discussion of the different ordinances we occasionally mentioned parallels from the New Testament. We shall endeavor now to integrate and summarize these parallels and as a result, to maintain our assumption that the first Christian community was also built upon a legal
code similar to the codes of the prevailing religious communities of its
time (231).
1) The designations of the community : The primitive Christian community is called κοινωνία and οἱ πολλοί (Acts of the Apostles 2:42; 1 Corinthians 10:16ff.), terms which are known to us from the Hellenistic world
and which are comparable to the יחד and the רבים in the Qumran sect.
In addition, the designations "Holy House" (בית קודש), "Holy Abode"
(מעון קודש) of the Sect which we find in 1QS 8:5ff., are reflected in the
Epistle to the Ephesians 2:21, where we find the Christian church termed : ναὸς ἅγιος, compare too 1 Corinth. 3:16; 1 Pet. 2:5.
2) The council of twelve in the primitive Christian community (Acts 1:
15ff.) is likewise known from the Qumran sect. As mentioned, the source
of this institution is to be found in the ancient organizational milieu.
3) The Bishop (Episkopus) is equivalent to the פקיד and to the מבקר
of the Qumran writings and is moreover found in the Hellenistic communities (above, pp. 19ff.).
4) The joint participation in property which is so typical of the Essene
sect typifies also the primitive Christian community (Acts 2:44-45; 4:
32), and the ordinances against lying in connection with property in
1QS 6:24-25 and in CD 14:11, 20 are reflected in the story of Ananias
and Sapphira in Acts 5:1ff. However, the punishment in the Christian
community is described as coming from the heavens.
5) The phraseology of lot-casting in connection with the selection of candidates is known from the Sect's writings (1QS 5:3, 6:16, 18, 22, 9:7,
CD 13:4, 12) and we find a similar matter, with similar language, in the
Acts of the Apostles. Of Judas Iscariot it is told that he was numbered
with the twelve and *acquired his position by lot* (ἔλαχεν τὸν κλῆρον
τῆς διακονίας ταύτης; Acts 1:17). In his stead Matthew is chosen in
order to take the office of ministry and to go to the place where he be-

---

231 Some of these parallels were discussed by J. Fitzmyer, Studies in Luke-Acts,
Essays Presented in Honor of P. Schubert (eds. L.E. Reck and J.L. Martyn),
1966, pp. 233ff. = *Essays on the Semitic Background of the New Testament*,
1971, pp. 271ff. However, Fitzmyer limits himself to parallels between the Qumran sect and the New Testament, and does not refer to the religious associations
of the Greco-Roman world.

longed (πορευθῆναι εἰς τὸν τόπον τὸν ἴδιον; vs. 25). As we saw above (p.25), the notion of τόπος ἴδιος was prevalent in the Hellenistic communities and indicated the position of a member according to his rank, a matter given expression in 1QS 2:23 : "And no one may rise from the place of his lot" (compare 2:22, 6:10, 22).

6) The communal meal which we find in the primitive Christian church (Acts 2:46) (232) was practiced not only in the Qumran sect (1QS 6:4-5, 1QSa 2:11-22), but also in the Pharisaic sect (233) and in the various Hellenistic communities.

7) The concern for the needs of members, particularly those of the widow, in the primitive Christian community (Acts 6:1ff.) is typical to the different communities, expecially those of Egypt, and is found also in the Damascus Covenant (6:20ff., 14:12ff.).

8) As in the Qumran scrolls (1QS 5:24ff., CD 7:2, 9:6-8), so also in the New Testament writings we find the warning to reprove one another and not to bear a grudge. If this reproof proves ineffective one must bring witnesses, and if this also is to no avail, the matter is brought before the Assembly (Matthew 18:16ff.). A similar procedure was found in the ordinances of the Iobacchi. Likewise, we find in Matthew 5:25 a parallel to the codes of the communities in the matter of insult and ridicule of members.

9) In the various codes it is forbidden to a member to apply to a court outside of the association. Similarly we find in the first Epistle to the Corinthians 6:11ff. a warning not to bring the brothers to judgment "before unbelievers".

10) Accepting new members, testing candidates and also a fixed trial periods for them, as found in the primitive Christian tradition (234), were practiced not only in the Qumran sect but also in the different Hellenistic communities which preceded them.

11) Jesus was considered in the Christian community as the founder of the community, similar to the "Teacher of Righteousness" of the Qumran sect and to the κτίστης in the Hellenistic communities.

These parallels show us that we cannot speak of the influences of the Sect on Christianity or *vice versa*, (235) since the religious associations of Ptolemaic Egypt and of the Hellenistic and Roman world were likewise based on similar ordinances. We have before us then, the accepted

---

232 Compare the Christian ἀγάπη, compare to the Pharisaic communal meal called מרעות (BMoed Qatan 22b), and see G. Alon, *Studies in Jewish History* I, p. 288 (Hebrew).
233 See Alon, *ibid.*, pp. 286ff.
234 Cf. below p. 70.
235 As does J.F. Baer in *Zion* 29 (1964), pp. 1-60 (Hebrew).

practice of establishing guilds and associations in those times. There is also no place for the claim that this practice started in Greece and penetrated to Palestine in the Hellenistic period because we find religious cultic associations already in the Persian period and even before that (cf. מרזח). As we have shown elsewhere, the pact of Nehemiah must be perceived as the code of the returnees from the Exile (236). Thus for example the "wood offering" (קרבן העצים) which we first find in the declaration of Nehemiah (Neh. 10:35) is an obligation well-known to us from the Hellenistic religious associations (ξυλωνία) (237).

---

236 See my article in *VT* 23 (1973), pp. 72ff.
237 See F. Poland, *Vereinswesen*, pp. 258, n. 2, 466; H.C. Youtie, "The Kline of Sarapis", *HThR* 41 (1948), pp. 22-23; cf. now the clause about supplying firewood in the Attic club, A.E. Raubitschek, 'A New Attic Club (ERANOS)', *The J. Paul Getty Museum Journal* 9 (1981), line 42 (p. 94).

APPENDIX A

I. The Statutes of the Iobacchi (178 CE)
(Dittenberger Sylloge [3] 1109)

"To good luck. In the archonship of Arrius Epaphroditus, on the eighth day of the month Elaphebolion, a meeting was convened for the first time by the priest who had been nominated by Aurelius Nicomachus, who had served as vice-priest for seventeen years and as priest for twenty-three years and had in his lifetime resigned his position, for the honour and glory of the Bacchic Society, in favour of the most excellent Claudius Herodes.

Nicomachus, nominated by Herodes as vice-priest, read aloud the statutes drawn up by the ex-priests, Chrysippus and Dionysius, and after the priest and the arch-bacchus and the patron had expressed their approval there were shouts of 'These are what we always observe,' 'Hurrah for the Priest !', 'Revive the statutes : you ought to,' 'Long life to the Bacchic Society, and good order !', 'Engrave the statutes,' 'Put the question.' The priest then said : 'Since my colleagues and I and all of you agree, we shall put the question as you demand.' Then the chairman, Rufus son of Aphrodisius, put the question : 'Whoever wishes the statutes which have been read to be ratified and engraved on a column will raise his hand.' All hands were raised. There were shouts of 'Long life to the most excellent priest Herodes !', 'Now you are in fortune : now we are the first of all Bacchic Societies,' 'Hurrah for the vice-priest !', 'Let the column be made !' The vice-priest said : 'The column shall rest upon the pillar, and the statutes shall be engraved; the officers will take care to prevent any infringement of them.'"

Then follows the text of the statutes thus ratified, in these terms :

"No one may be an Iobacchus unless he is first registered in the usual manner with the priest and is approved by a vote of the Iobacchi as being clearly worthy and fit to be a member of the Bacchic Society.

The entrance-fee shall be fifty denarii and a libation for one who is not the son of a member, while the sons of members shall lodge a similar notice and pay, in addition to twenty-five denarii, half the usual subscription until the attainment of puberty.

The Iobacchi shall meet on the ninth of each month and on the anniversary of its foundation and on the festivals of Bacchus and on any extraordinary feast of the god, and each member shall take part in word or act or honourable deed, paying the fixed monthly contribution for the wine. If he fail to pay, he shall be excluded from the gathering and this exclusion shall be enforced by those whose names are recorded in the decree, save in case of absence from home or mourning or illness or if he who is to be admitted to the gathering was under some strong compulsion, of which the priests are to judge.

And if the brother of an Iobacchus enter the Society after approval by vote, he shall pay fifty denarii; but if any acolyte living outside pay the sums due to the gods and to the Bacchic Society, he shall be an Iobacchus together with his father, sharing with his father in a single libation.

When anyone has lodged his application and has been approved by vote, the priest shall hand him a letter stating that he is an Iobacchus, but not until he has first paid to the priest his entrance fee, and in the letter the priest shall cause to be entered the sums paid under one head or another.

No one may either sing or create a disturbance or applaud at the gathering, but each shall say and act his allotted part with all good order and quietness under the direction of the priest or the arch-bacchus.

No Iobacchus who has not paid his contributions for the monthly and anniversary meetings shall enter the gathering until the priests have decided either that he must pay or that he may be admitted.

If anyone start a fight or be found acting disorderly or occupying the seat of any other member or using insulting or abusive language to anyone, the person so abused or insulted shall produce two of the Iobacchi to state upon oath that they heard him insulted or abused, and he who was guilty of the insult or abuse shall pay to the Society twenty-five light drachmas, or he who was responsible for the fight shall pay the same sum of twenty-five drachmas, on pain of exclusion from the meetings of the Iobacchi until they make payment.

And if anyone come to blows, he who has been struck shall lodge a written statement with the priest or the vice-priest, and he shall without fail convene a general meeting, and the Iobacchi shall decide the question by vote under the presidency of the priest, and the penalty shall be exclusion for a period to be determined and a fine not exceeding twenty-five silver dernarii.

And the same punishment shall be imposed also on one who, having been struck, fails to seek redress with the priest or the arch-bacchus but has brought a charge before the public courts.

And the same punishment shall be imposed upon the orderly officer (εὔκοσμος) if he failed to eject those who were fighting.

And if any of the Iobacchi, knowing that a general meeting ought to be convened for this purpose, fail to attend, he shall pay to the Society fifty light drachmas, and if he fail to pay on demand, the treasurer shall have power to prevent him from entering the Bacchic Society until he pay.

And if any of those who enter fail to pay the entrance-fee to the priest or to the vice-priest, he shall be excluded from the banquet until he does pay, and the money shall be exacted in whatsoever way the priest may order.

And no one shall deliver a speech without the permission of the priest or of the vice-priest on pain of being liable to a fine of thirty light drachmas to the Society.

The priest shall perform the customary services at the meeting and the anniversary in proper style, and shall set before the meeting the drink-offering for the return of Bacchus (τὰ καταγώγια) and pronounce the sermon, which Nicomachus the ex-priest inaugurated as an act of public spirit.

And the arch-bacchus shall offer the sacrifice to the god and shall set forth the drink-offering on each tenth day of the month Elaphebolion.

And when portions are distributed, let them be taken by the priest, vice-priest, arch-bacchus, treasurer, bucolicus, Dionysus, Core, Palaemon, Aphrodite and Proteurythmus; and let these names be apportioned by lot among all the members.

And if any of the Iobacchi receive any legacy or honour or appointment, he shall set before the Iobacchi a drink-offering corresponding to the appointment, — marriage, birth, Choes, coming of age (ἐφηβεία), citizen-status, the office of wand-bearer, councillor, president of the games, Panhellen, elder, thesmothetes, or any magistracy whatsoever, the appointment as συνθύτης or as justice of the peace, the title of ἱερονείκης, or any other promotion attained by any Iobacchus.

The orderly officer shall be chosen by lot or appointed by the priest, and he shall bear the thyrsus of the god to him who is disorderly or creates a disturbance. And anyone beside whom the thyrsus is laid shall, with the approval of the priest or of the arch-bacchus, leave the banqueting-hall : but if he disobey, the 'horses' who shall be appointed by the priests shall take him up and put him outside the front door and he shall be liable to the punishment inflicted upon those who fight.

The Iobacchi shall elect a treasurer (ταμίας), by ballot (ψῆφος) for a term of two years, and he shall take over all the property of the Bacchic Society in accordance with an inventory, and shall likewise hand it over to his successor as treasurer.

And he shall provide out of his own pocket the oil for the lights on each ninth day of the month and on the anniversary and at the assembly and on all the customary days of the god and on those days when legacies or honours or appointments are celebrated.

And he shall, if he wish, appoint a secretary at his own risk, and he shall be allowed the treasurer's drink-offering and shall be free from the payment of subscriptions for the two years.

And if any Iobacchus die, a wreath shall be provided in his honour not exceeding five denarii in value, and a single jar of wine shall be set before those who have attended the funeral; but anyone who has not attended may not partake of the wine."

II.Sections of the Iobacchi code paralleled with the Qumran regulations

Iobacchi Code

Qumran Sect

1.

"Anyone of Israel who dedicates himself to join the council of the community the 'officer in charge of Many' (הפקיד ברואש הרבים) shall inquire as to *his mind and his deeds* (לשכלו ולמעשיו)... Later when

"No one may be a Iobacchus unless he is first registered in the usual manner with the priest and is approved by the vote of the Iobacchi as being clearly worthy and fit to be a member of the Bacchic society."

he comes to stand before the Many; they shall all be asked concerning his affairs and according to the lot as comes forth from the council of the Many he shall either be accepted or rejected" (יקרב או ירחק) (1Q S 6:14 ff.).

"And anyone who is joining the congregation let him be checked as to his actions, his mind, his strength, his valor and his property, and they shall register him in his place according to his status *in the lot of the light*" (בגורל האור) (CD 13:11-12). Compare 1Q S 5:10 ff.

2.

"No one must speak in the middle of the speech of another member, (thus interrupting) before he has finished talking. Nor must he speak before the rank of the one who is enlisted before him (in the hierarchy)... At a session of the Many nobody must say anything which is not according to the will of the Many" (1Q S 6:10-11).

"No one may either sing or create a disturbance or applaud at the gathering, but each shall say and act his allotted part with all good order and quietness under the direction of the priest or the arch-bacchus."

"The one who interrupts his colleague's speech his fine will be ten day. The one who lies down and falls asleep at a session of the Many (shall be fined) for thirty days, and the same applies to the man who leaves the session of the Many... The man who spits into the session of the Many shall be fined for thirty days..." (1QS 7:9-13).

"According to his word (the overseer's) shall the members of the congregation come, each man in his turn" (CD 14:10).
Compare :
"No clamour or disturbance ever pollutes the house, they speak in turn each making way for his neighbor" (BJ II, 132).

3.
If anyone start a fight or be found acting disorderly or occupying the seat of any other member or using insulting or abusive language to anyone, the person so abused or insulted shall produce two of the Iobacchi to state upon oath that they heard him insulted or abused, and he who was guilty of the insult or abuse shall pay to the Society twenty-five drachmas... and if anyone come to blows, he who has been struck shall lodge a written statement with the priest or the vice priest, and he shall without fail convene a general meeting, and the Iobacchi shall decide the

"And the one who answer his neighbour with a stiff neck and speaks with fury... against the word of his neighbor who is enlisted before him... shall be fined one year..." (1 QS 6:26-27).

"the one who gets angry at his comrade shall be fined for six months; the one who scoffs wantonly at his neighbor... shall be fined for one year and shall be put into confinement; the one who speaks to his neighbor with arrogance or plays false with his comrade shall be fined for six months" (1 QS 7:3-5).

"nor must anyone bring up any case against his neighbor before

question by vote under the
presidency of the priest, and
the penalty shall be exclusion for
a period to be determined...

the Many without proof before
witnesses" (1 QS 6:1).

"everyone of the members of the
covenant who brings against his
neighbor an accusation without
reproving before witnesses... he is
one who takes vengeance and bears
rancour" (CD 9:24).

"if your brother commits a sin, go
and take the matter up with him
strictly between yourselves.. if he
will not listen, take one or two
others with you, so that all facts
may be duly established on the evidence of two or three witnesses.
If he refuses to listen to them, report the matter to the congregation" (Matth. 18:15 ff.).

4.
"If any of the Iobacchi, knowing
that a general meeting ought
to be convened for this purpose,
fail to attend, he shall pay to the
society fifty light drachmas..."

"and the same punishment (thirty
days) applies to the man who leaves
the session of the Many without
permission and wantonly up to
three times at a session, he shall
be fined for ten days; if they should
hold a vote and he leaves, then he
shall be fined for thirty days"
(1 QS 7:10-12).

5.
"and no one shall deliver a
speech without the permission
of the priest or the vice priest..."

"Anyone who has something to
say to the Many... shall get up on
his feet and say : 'I have something
to say to the Many'. If they say to
him ("speak") then he may speak"
(1QS 6:10-13).

APPENDIX B

THE EIN-GEDI COMMUNITY

I

The mosaic floor of the synagogue in Ein-Gedi (1) is unique, as among the lines of the brief dedication to the memory of the sons of Hilfi (l. 9-10, 17-18), there appears a passage which constitutes a sort of charter incumbent upon all the inhabitants of the village. They are prohibited against fostering division among the townspeople, against slandering a fellow guild-member to the Gentiles, against stealing from a brother or revealing the "secret of the city" (*raza de-qarta*).

These regulations are backed by Divine sanction :

כל מן ... דין דעינוה משוטטן בכל ארעה
וחמי סתירתה הוא יתן אפוה בגברה
ההו ובזרעיה ויעקור יתיה מן תחות שומיה
וימרון כל עמה אמן ואמן סלה

Whoever (shall do one of these things) ... He whose eyes run to and fro through the whole earth
And who sees the concealed, He will set His face on that man
And on his seed, and will uproot him from under the heavens
And all the people shall say : Amen and Amen Selah.

Students of this inscription have already noted that the "secret of the town" was related to the expertise of the people of Ein-Gedi in growing spices, and that this oath or regulation is to be viewed in this context (2). However, as no similar charters of craft-guilds for this period have been found, nor similar formulations, some doubts have been raised concerning this (3). We shall discuss below oaths of loyalty to one's employers, whose structure is similar to that of this document, as well as

------

1   B. Mazar, "The Inscription on the Floor of the Synagogue in En-Gedi — Preliminary Survey" (Heb.), *Tarbiz* 40 (1971), pp. 18-23 and, more recently, J. Naveh, *'al Pesifas va-even* (On Stone and Mosaic — The Aramaic and Hebrew Inscriptions from Ancient Synagogues (Heb.)), (Tel-Aviv, Jerusalem, 1978), inscription no. 70, pp. 107-109.
2   See the articles by B. Mazar, S. Lieberman and E.E. Urbach in *Tarbiz, art. cit.*
3   See e.g., B. Lifschitz, "The Ancient Synagogue of Hamat-Tiberias, its Floor and Inscription" (Heb.), in *Mehqarim betoldot 'Am Yisra'el ve-Erez Yisra'el* 3 (1975), pp. 107-109.

similar regulations for various kinds of associations. This being the case, it seems that here too we find a charter for individuals who belonged to a common craft-guild.

In this inscription there is a kind of dialogue : adjuration or administration of the oath by the head of the community, followed by the taking of the oath by the members of the community. First, the conditions to which they are swearing are specified, and then the oath is ratified by the members of the congregation : "And all the people say : Amen Amen Selah." This latter phrase is reminiscent of the ratification of the covenant by the members of the *yaḥad* in Qumran : "And all who have been admitted to the covenant shall say after them in response, Amen Amen'" (*Manual of Discipline* 2:18) (4).

A similar dialogue appears in the oath of loyalty of artisans and smiths from the Persian period, discovered at Erech (5). There, the heads of the Temple of Eanna in Erech address the craftsmen (smelters and the like), saying : (ll.18ff.) "(You may make re)pairs involving silver, gold (6)... (If) you do not do the work and you do not make repairs and... (if someone) does work or make repairs (in) another temple, (he shall suffer punishment...)." The craftsmen and smiths reply : (ll. 24-25) N(o on)e ... will do work or make repairs i(n the te)mples of the town

---

4   See : BT, Shevu'ot 29b; "Samuel said : 'Whoever answers "Amen" after an oath is as if he himself had made that oath, as is written, "And the woman shall answer : 'Amen Amen.'" (Num. 5:22).'" Cf. *Ibid.* 36a : "'Amen' —— there is an oath, there is an accepting of the things, there is confirmation of the words.'" Further on, Rabba states that the ratification of the oath is dependent upon the repetition of the word "Yes." Cf. Deut. R. 7:1. "This 'Amen' entails three אספליאות : oath, acceptance and ratification." On the term *aspliyah* (Gk., ἀσφά-λεια = surety) see : S. Lieberman, *Greek in Jewish Palestine*, New York, (1942), p. 8; and H. J. Polotsky, "Three Greek Documents from the Family Archive of Babatha" (Heb.), in *Eretz Israel* 8 (*E. L. Sukenik Memorial Volume*), (1967), pp. 46-47, Document no. 12, l. 9 (interior), l. 12 (exterior), and the commentary, *ibid.*, p. 49.

5   D.B. Weisberg, *Guild Structure and Political Allegiance in Early Achaemenid Mesopotamia*, (New Haven, 1967), pp. 5ff., although there we are not speaking of a "charter" of a group of autonomous craftsmen, as Weisberg argues, but of artisans who are subject to the authorities of the Temple. On this, see : J. Renger, *JAOS* 91 (1971), pp. 494ff.

6   *bat-q(u ta-ṣab-ba-ta u dul-lu) ša KU. BABBAR... te-ip-pu-ša* (l.18ff.) *batqa ṣabātu* (to strengthen the breach) and *dulla epēšu* (to do labor) appear in the context of repairs (see: *CAD*, vid., *batqu; ṣabātu* 8) and overlap the Hebrew *ḥzq*, *bdq* and *' śh ml'kh* in the context of Temple repairs in II K. 12:6ff. and II K. 22:5. In later books, we find the term *hḥzq* instead of *ḥzq*. Thus, in Ezek. 27:9, 27, we find מחזיקי בדקך instead of מחזקי בדקך and in Neh. 3 *hḥzq* (more than thirty times) in the sens of repair (see *BDB*, s. v., חזק 4). In light of this, and particularly in light of the expression "repair and do" (*ṣabātu & epēšu*) in the oath of allegiance from Babylonia, it seems to me that that one should interpret the phrase from the synagogue in Susia (Naveh, *op. cit.* (n.1) no. 76), שהחזיקו ועשו in the sense of repaired (although I do not think that one can apply this same sense to *'thzq* in other inscriptions).

(or the) cult-centers (or) anyplace what(soever with)out our permis(sion). Nor (ll. 25-27) shall we conceal or keep secret anything which we see or hear whenever (some)one does w(ork) else(where)."

The injunction against performing labor in another temple may be explained in several different ways : a fear of profanation of the material intended for use at the temple of Eanna, the desire to bind the crafts-men to this specific task, etc. (7). However, the most significant factor was without doubt the desire to preserve the trade secrets entailed in the specific plans of the temple (8). We find this type of secrecy in the docu-ment under discussion as well (see below).

II

A similar pattern of adjuration and oath-taking appears in the oath of Asaph the Physician, recently discussed by S. Pines (9). There, too, we find that the physicians Asaph and Yohanan adjure their students, after which the students themselves take an oath. Among the sanctions stated there : "You shall not speak of the herbs (out of which such drugs are made). You shall not hand them over to any man, and you shall not talk about any matter (connected) with this" (ll. 49-50). Likewise, in the Hippocratic oath —— to which the oath of Asaph the Physician is connec-ted, and from which it may have borrowed (10) —— the one who takes the oath is required to teach the science of healing only to those "who have taken an oath according to the medical law, and to no one else" (ll. 9-10) (11).

This insistence that one not reveal professional medical secrets is also mentioned in a collection of documents of Hippocrates (12). For example, at the end of *Decorum,* it is stated that the physician must carefully pre-serve the science of healing and teach it to another (within his fraternity), because praiseworthy things are guarded well by such people (13). At the

7   See : Weisberg, *op. cit.* (n. 5), p. 37-38, and Renger, *op. cit.* (n. 5).
8   See : Weisberg, *ibid.,* p. 37. On this subject, compare what is related concerning Bet-Avtinas, that they did not wish to teach their skill to others (M. Yoma 3:11; BT Yoma 38a; JT Yoma 3:9 (41a); Shekalim 5:2 (48d), and below p. 54.
9   S. Pines, "The Oath of Asaph the Physician and Yohanan ben Zabda," *Procee-dings of the Israel Academy of Sciences of Humanities* V, (1975), pp. 223-262.
10 Pines, *ibid.*
11 Pines, *ibid.,* p. 260 (text according to Edelstein), sec. 2. (English translation : pp. 228-229).
12 W. H. S. Jones, tr.,*Hippocrates,* I-II, (The Loeb Classical Library) (London, 1923).
13 See Jones, *op. cit.,* II p. 300, and his comments concerning the cryptic nature of these instructions.

conclusion of the *Nomos*, it states : "Things however that are holy are revealed only to men who are holy. The profane may not learn them until they have been initiated into the mysteries of science" (14).

We also find warnings of this kind in medical texts from Mesopotamia. Thus, for example, in a medical text we read (15) : "Let the initiated (lit. 'knower') show the secrets of the magical experts to the initiated; the uninitiated shall not see them; regarding the son (16) whom you favor, make him swear by the name of Asalluḫi and Ninurta, then show him..."

Likewise, in a colophon to a medical text we find (17) : "Ointments and bandages tested and checked ... the one who is not expert should show to the expert, the expert shall not show to the one who is not expert" (18).

The preservation of professional secrecy and its transmission to others under oath is not confined to medicine. Thus, for example, it is told of Bet-Avtinas, a closed family of craftsmen during the Second Temple period, that one of the members of the family told someone who had been asked to be shown a certain herb : "It is an oath in our hands, that it is not shown to any man (19). Josephus writes of the Essenes, who apparently practiced medicine, that they had taken an oath not to conceal anything from other members of the sect, but not to reveal their secrets to outsiders. They had likewise sworn to pass on the rules as they had received them *(BJ* II:141-142) (20). All this indicates that various sects and guilds were bound to their rules, which included clauses assuring the preservation of secrecy.

The maintenance of secrecy of course depends upon the unity or cohesion of the members and the maintenance of strict internal discipline. Therefore, the regulations of these closed societies contain warnings against division or disputes, against slander and the bringing of complaints

14 Jones, *ibid.,* pp. 264-5, sec. 5. On the special language, characteristic of closed groups, found here, see : W.H.S. Jones, *The Doctor's Oath* (Cambridge, 1925), p. 46, no. 1.
15 E.K. Ritter, in *Studies in honor of Benno Landsberger* (Oriental Institute of the University of Chicago. Assyriological Studies 16. (Chicago, 1965)), p. 301 (*KAR* 230:10ff.) : *niṣirti āšipūti mudû mudâ likallim, lā mudû lā immar; ana mārika ša tarammu šum ᵈAsalluḫi u ᵈNinurta šuskirma kullimšu.*
16 The Hippocratic Oath also speaks of the passing on of knowledge to the "sons" in the sense of students; Cf. my article, "The Genuine Jewish Attitude Towards Abortion" (Heb.), in *Zion* 42 (1978), p. 135, n. 39.
17 R.C. Thompson, *Assyrian medical texts...* (London, New York, 1923), No. 105, iv : 21-25.
18 *ᵐnapšalatu (< pašāšu) takṣirānu latkūtu barûti... lā mudû mudâ likallim mudû la mudû lā ikallim';* cf. H. Hunger, *Babylonische und assyrische Kolophone,* (AOAT 2 (1968)), no. 533, p. 142.
19 BT Yoma 38a and parallels.
20 For secret physiognomical writings of the Qumran sect, see J. Licht, "Legs as Sign of Election" (Heb.), *Tarbiz* 35 (1966), pp. 18-26.

to outside groups, as expressed in the inscription under discussion. Thus, for example, in the code of the guild of Zeus Hypsistos (Papyrus London) we read (21) : "And he shall not cause dispute ... and not gossip (22) nor complain nor blame his fellow (before the court) (23).

Similar clauses appear in the regulations of Egyptian associations, written in Demotic. These contain expressions such as : *dj.t bjn* —— "to do (i.e., speak) evil" and *smj.r* —— "complain" (24) before the authorities (25). S. Lieberman has rightfully argued that the adjuration in the Ein-Gedi inscription not to speak evil to the Gentiles refers to conveying information to the authorities (26). A similar idea is expressed in an oath of loyalty to the Holy Fellowship from the Geonic period, in which the member swears not to betray the *yeshiva* or the *haburah* "and not to derogate any person from Israel, and not to open my mouth... to mention with contempt any of the inhabitants of Jerusalem or like them the people of the *yeshiva* and their fellows, and that I shall from now on and forever love those who love our master Daniel, the great prince, the head of the *yeshiva*, the pride of Jacob... and hate those who hate him" (27). The text in this oath concerning loving those who love the master and hating those that hate him is extremely ancient, appearing in oaths of loyalty in the ancient Near East (28), as does the expression "from now on and forever" (29). The warning in the code of the Ein-Gedi community against one who steals his neighbor's property has parallels in the regulations of the Qumran *yahad* as well as in the regulations of other associations in the Hellenistic period (30).

We have thus established basic points of similarity between the regulations of the Ein-Gedi community and those of various kinds of professional and religious societies known to us from the Hellenistic and Roman periods.

---

21   C. Roberts, T. Skeat, A.D. Nock, "The Guild of Zeus Hypsistos", *Harvard Theological Review* 29 (1936), pp. 39ff.

22   λαλῆσειν. It is possible that the intent here is that one should not speak of the matters of the group outside of the group itself, in which case this idea is parallel to the revealing of the secret in our case. In light of what we now know about the strictness with which the secrets of the group were kept, there is no justification for the editors' doubts (p. 53) concerning this interpretation.

23   Ll. 16-17 and cf. above p. 37.

24   See references and discussion in : F. de Cenival, *Les associations religieuses en Egypte d'après les documents démotiques*, (Le Caire, 1972), p.54, cf. above p. 36.

25   On the prohibitaion against appeal to outside courts in the codes of guilds in the Hellenistic-Roman world, see above p. 34.

III

The similarity among these regulations is not only expressed in the contents of their individual clauses, but in their structure as well. We have seen that the dialogic structure of adjuration on the part of the one administering the oath, and oath-taking by those undertaking the obligation which is reflected in the inscription under discussion here, also appears in oaths and charters of professional associations. In fact, these are anchored in contracts and oaths of loyalty from the second millennium B.C.E. (31). However, we must mention two additional contractual elements found in the Ein-Gedi inscription, and known to us from treaties and loyalty-oaths from the ancient Near East : witnesses and the curse.

The appeal to witnesses of a heavenly, eternal character, in order to lend force to the oath, is known to us from documents of the ancient Near East (32). It would appear that the invocation of the Patriarchs (33) and the constellations (34) at the beginning of the Ein-Gedi inscription are intended as witnesses to the oath that follows thereafter (35). Likewise, Philo of Alexandria states that the oath must be made in the name of the progenating fathers, as well as in the name of the earth, the heavens and the stars (*On Laws* II, 1) (36). The appeal to witnesses is also found both in the oath of the students of Hippocrates (37) and in that of the students of Asaph the Physician (38).

————

26 "A Preliminary Remark to the Inscription of En-Gedi" (Heb.), *Tarbiz* 40 (1971), pp. 25-26.
27 S. Schechter, *Saadyana*, (Cambridge, 1903), Doc. No. XLII, p. 114. On the organization of the *yeshiva* and *ḥaburah* along the lines of a guild, see above p.28.
28 See my article, "The Loyalty Oath in the Ancient Near East," *Ugarit Forschungen* 8 (1976), pp. 390-391.
29 See : S.E. Loewenstamm, "'From this Time forth and for Evermore'" (Heb.), *Tarbiz* 32 (1963), p. 313ff., and references there.
30 See above p. 38.
31 See my article, *op. cit.* (n. 28).
32 *Ibid.*
33 On the "fathers of the world" and the "pillars of the world" (Abraham Isaac and Jacob, or Hananiah, Mishael and Azariah) in this inscription, see Mazar (quoting Urbach), *Tarbiz* 40 (1971), pp. 22-23.
34 Compare this introduction to the treaty of Essarhadon with the vassals, l. 13ff. : "and before the planets Jupiter, Venus, Saturn, etc."; see my article in *Ug. Forsch.* 8 (above n. 28), p. 397, n. 169.
35 Mazar, *ibid.*, pp. 22-23, correctly sensed that in mentioning the fathers of the nation the author referred to an oath.
36 See my article (n. 28), p. 397.
37 The oath is taken by Apollo, Asclepius, and by *all the gods and goddesses*. The latter formula appears in pagan treaties beginning in the 2nd millennium B.C.E. See my article (n.28), pp. 396-397.
38 "Behold, the Lord God and his saints and His Torah are witnesses before you" (1. 46). My attention was drawn to this matter by Dr. A. Lieber, who is now preparing a scientific edition of the Oath of Asaph. In her opinion, this text includes two different versions of the oath, each one of which contains an address to witnesses (invocatio).

The curse found in our inscription : "... against that man and his seed, and uproot him from under the heavens," is a stereotyped curse appearing in many treaties and oaths (39), explained by the Sages as follows : "All violations of the Torah are taken out against him here (in the false oath) *against him and his family*" (BT Shevu'ot 39a). The uprooting of the violator from underneath the heavens reminds us of the lot of the violator of the covenant in Deut. 29:19-20 : "The Lord shall blot out his name from under heaven. And the Lord shall separate him for evil out of all the tribes of Israel, according to all the curses of the covenant that are written in this book of the law" (40).

A curse in the spirit of Deut. 29:19 also appears in the *Manual of Discipline* : "God shall set him apart for misfortune, and he shall be cut off from the midst of all the children of light... God will set his lot among those that are accurses for ever !" (1QS 2:16-17), followed by the sentence : "And all who have been admitted to the covenant shall say after them in response, Amen, amen" (1. 18), parallel to the sentence in the document under discussion here "And all the people shall say : Amen Amen Selah" (1. 16), which also follows the curse (41).

The various pieces of evidence we have cited strengthens the conclusion that we are speaking here of an oath administered by the people of the town to the heads of the craft guild (of spice-makers), Yosa, 'Ezron, and Hizzikiyyo. This oath was preserved for posterity within the mosaic made by the members of the guild in memory of its leaders and founders (42).

39 See my article, (n. 28), pp. 397-398.
40 For parallel motifs in curses in Ancient Near Eastern treaties, see my book : *Deuteronomy and the Deuteronomic School*, pp. 107-108.
41 See above, note 4.
42 On the importance of the founder of the guild (κτίστης) and the preservation of his name after his death, see : M. San Nicolo, *Aegyptisches Vereinswesen zur Zeit der Ptolomäer und Römer*, II, pp. 7ff. (Compare also above, p.45). On κτίστης in Jewish documents, see : B. Lifschitz, *Donateurs et fondateurs dans les synagogues juives*, (1967), No. 81b, pp. 72-73.

APPENDIX C

Adjuration of a Jewish-Christian sect concerning the non-communication of the sacred books to any one of the Gentiles or to any one not initiated

(Epistle of Peter to James in the Pseudo-Clementine Literature)

B. Rehm, *Die Pseudoklementinen, Homilien I* (Die griechischen-christlichen Schriftsteller 42) 1953, pp. 1-4; *The Clementine Homilies* Ante-Nicene Christian Library (ed. A. Roberts, S. Donaldson) 1870, pp. 1-5.

_____

"I beseech you not communicate to any one of the Gentiles the books of my preachings which I sent to you nor to any one of our own tribe before testing; but if any one has been examined and found worthy (ἄξιος), then transmit them to him after the manner in which Moses transmitted (παρέδωκε) (the Torah) to the seventy (1) who succeeded to his chair (καθέδραν) (2)...

In order, therefore, that the like may also happen to those among us as to these seventy give the books of my preachings to our brethren in the way of initiation into mystery (covenant) (3) that they may teach those who wish to take part in learning, for if it be not so done our word of truth will be rent into many opinions...

Therefore, that no such thing may happen, for this end I have prayed and besought you not to communicate the books of my preaching which I have sent you to any one, whether of our nation or of another nation before testing; but if any one, having been examined, has been found worthy, then hand them over to him, according to the initiation (ἀγωγή) (4) of Moses, by which he delivered (the Torah) to the seventy who succeeded to his chair...

_____

1   In accordance with the Rabbinic concept attested in Mishna Abot 1:1 : 'Moses *received* (קבל) the Torah from Sinai and transmitted (מסר) it to Joshua and Joshua to the elders'. קבלה and מסירה correspond to παραλαμβάνω and παραδίδωμι prevalent in connection with handing down oral and written tradition in Jewish-Hellenistic sources.

2   The *cathedra* of Moses on which the Pharisees professed to sit (Matt.23:2) is mentioned in Rabbinic literature (Pesikta d'Rab Kahana 7, ed. Mandelbaum, p.12) and signifies the chair of the Rabbi-preacher in the synagogue (cf. E.L. Sukenik, *Tarbiz* I, 1 (1929), pp. 145ff.).

3   τῆς ἀγωγῆς μυστήριον. Philo (Virt. 33, 178) describes the entrance into the covenant in Deut. 29:11-14 as initiation into a mystery-sect (μυσταγωγῶν), cf. my article 'The Loyalty Oath in the Ancient Near East', *Ugarit-Forschungen* 8 (1976) p. 407, note 256.

4   See note 3.

Adjuration

1. Therefore James, having read the epistle, sent for ehe elders (presbyters) and having read it to them said :

> 'Our Peter has strictly and becomingly charged us concerning the establishing of the truth, that we should not communicate the books of his preachings, which have been sent to us, to any one by chance, but to one who is good and devout and who wishes to teach and who is circumcised and faithful. And these are not all to be transmitted to him at once... let him be examined not less than six years. And then according to the initiation (ἀγωγή) of Moses, he (that is to transmit the books) should bring him to a river or a fountain (5), which is living water, where the regeneration (6) of the righteous takes place and should make him not swear — for that is not lawful — but to stand by the water and conjure, as we ourselves when we were regenerated, were made to do for the sake of not sinning.'

2. And let him say : 'I take to witness heaven, earth, water, in which all things are comprehended, and in addition to all these, that air also which pervades all things, and without which I cannot breathe, that I shall always be obedient to him who gives me the books of the preachings; and those same books which he may give me, I shall not communicate to any one in any way, either by writing them, or giving them in writing, or giving them to a writer, either myself or by another, or through any other initiation, or trick, or method, or by keeping them carelessly, or placing them before (any one) or granting him permission (to see them), or in any way or manner whatsoever communicating them to another; unless I shall ascertain one to be worthy (ἄξιον) (as I myself have been judged, or even more so, and that after a probation of not less than six years); but to one who is religious and good, chosen to teach; as have received them, so I will transmit them, doing these things according to the will of my bishop...

And that I shall thus do, I again call to witness heaven, earth, water in which all things are enveloped, and in addition to all these, the all-pervading air, without which I cannot breathe, that I shall always be obdient to him who gives me these books of the preachings and shall

---

5   Rivers and fountains next to heaven and earth (which appear in the continuation of our adjuration) occur also as witnesses in treaty oaths of the ancient Near East and ancient Greece, cf. my article in *UF* 8 (1976), pp. 395-396.

6   For the imagery of the initiated into the mystery as *regenerated* cf. R. Reitzenstein, *Die hellenistischen Mysterienreligionen/3* 1927, pp. 262ff; compare 1 Sam. 10:6.

observe all the things I have been adjured, or even more. To me therefore keeping this covenant (τὰς ουνθήχας) there shall be a part with the holy ones (7).

But to me doing anything contrary to what I have covenanted (παρ᾽ ἃ ουνθέμην) may the universe be hostile to me, and the all-pervading ether, and the God who is over all, to whom none is superior, than whom none is greater...

And in addition to all these things, if I shall lie, I shall be accursed living and dying (8), and shall be punished with everlasting punishment.'

And after all this, let him partake of bread and salt with him who transmits them to him (9).

The adjuration is accepted

James said : "Hear me, brethren and fellow servants. If we should give the books to all indiscriminately, and they should be corrupted by any daring man, or be perverted by interpretations, as you have heard that some have already done, it will remain even for those who really seek the truth, always to wander in error. Wherefore it is better that they should be with us, and that we should communicate them with all the forementioned care to those who wish to live piously and to save others. But if any one after taking this adjuration shall act otherwise, he shall with good reason incur eternal punishment...".

As has been recognized by G. Strecker (10) we have to distinguish in this epistle between two layers : the kerygma of Peter and the adjuration (= the *contestatio*). The adjuration contains indeed elements which reflect sectarian comitments of esoteric nature. These elements are attested in all kinds of sects and esoteric groups discussed above. The system of adjuration by the head of the group followed by acceptance of the adjuration, i.e. taking an oath by the members of the group, which has been discusses above in connection with the En-Gedi inscription (p. 52f.), is also found here. First comes Peter's command and then the words of James and the elders pledging before eternal witnesses to fulfill the command. In the En-Gedi community we find the pledge not to reveal the secret of the town; here we find the pledge not to reveal the lore of the sacred books.

---

7   For the significance of communion with the holy ones in Qumran literature and the New Testament writings cf. my article 'The Heavenly Praise in Unison', *Meqor Ḥajjim*, Fest-schrift für G.Molin zum 75. Geburtstag, Graz 1983, pp.429ff.
8   For this sort of curse cf. my article in *Ugarit-Forschungen* 8 (1976), p. 399.
9   This expresses covenantal relationship, cf. my article ברית in *ThWAT* col. 791, and references there.
10 *Das Judenchristentum in den Pseudoklementinen*, Texte und Untersuchungen zur Geschichte der altchristlichen Literatur 70 (1958), pp. 137-144.

This injunction not to reveal the esoteric knowledge for the uninitiated, the unworthy (and the uncircumcized) reminds us the warnings of the Qumran sect to conceal the truth of the mysteries of knowledge (חבא לאמת רזי דעת IQS 4:6) or more explicitly : 'to conceal the Torahcounsel from the midst of the men of deceit' (ולסתר את עצת התורה בתוך אנשי העול IQS 9:17) which corresponds to what Josephus says about the Essenes that they swear ... carefully to preserve the books of the sect and the names of the angels' (BJ II 142).

A similar concept may be detected in the writings of Philo. Speaking about Moses' entering the tabernacle he says that only those who 'have put off all the things of creation ... are allowed to enter into the invisible region ... to learn the most sacred mysteries (τὰς ἱεροτάτας τελετάς), (De Gigantibus 53-54). In another place he says that when he talks about the virtues, those who corrupt religion should close their ears or depart, for it is a divine mystery, and its lesson is for the initiated who are worthy (ἄξιος) to receive the holiest secret (De Cherubim 42). He adds that he himself was initiated under Moses into his greater mysteries as a worthy minister of the holy secrets (ἱεροφάντης) (ibid. 49). This resembles the words of Peter in the epistle that only the worthy shall be given the books transmitted to him after the manner of Moses. This idea is to be found in the tradition of Greek philosophy where certain philosophical doctrines were considered mysteries which only the worthy are allowed to be taught (11).

The same idea is propagated in the Rabbinic cycles in connection with the teaching of the mysteries of Merkabah (12).

Similarly we find in the Egyptian Isis mystery described by Lucius Apuleius that he is not allowed to reveal what was said to him during his initiation (Metamorphoses XI, 23). More close to our source is the description of the Elkesaites (13) by Hippolytus (14). Hippolytus cites from the 'book of Elkesai' as follows : 'Do not recite this account to all men and guard carefully these precepts, because all men are not faithful...'

Some scholars considered this comand to be the source of the instruction of Peter in the epistle under scrutiny (15) but in the light of the material adduced above there is no justification for this supposition. It seems that most of the esoteric circles had such regulations which are close in nature to the ones cited above (p. 54) from the various guilds :

---

11 Cf. H.A. Wolfson, *Philo* I 1947, p. 54.
12 Wolfson, ibid., p. 55.
13 A Jewish-Christian sect which arose c. 100 CE in the area east of the Jordan.
14 *Refutation of all Heresies*, IX, 17, 1 (Die griechischen christlichen Schriftsteller der ersten drei Jahrhunderte, ed. Wendland).
15 Cf. Strecker's discussion in the book mentioned above note 10.

'Let the initiated show the secrets to the initiated, the uninitiated shall not see them.'

As indicated above the epistle discussed here reflects covenanted rules known to us from various mysteries and religious groups. Not only the central concern of the epistle i.e. preserving the secrecy of the holy books, is attested in various sects and esoteric groups, but also other features such as :

1) the examination of the candidates
2) probation (six years)
3) the formalities of the pledge taken by the members : standing at the river and the fountain and calling witnesses.
4) blessings and curses. The blessing for a common share with the angels is especially known to us from Qumran (see note 7). The curses are known to us from the various oaths and treaties.
5) bread and salt as a sign of covenant (see note).
6) initiation as regeneration (cf. note 6).
7) adjuration through dialogue : Peter's kerygma and James' and the elders' invocation (cf. above pp. 51ff.).

APPENDIX D

The Apostolic Tradition (Hippolytus) (cf. p. 44)

F.X. Funk, *Didascalia et Constitutiones Apostolorum*, Vol. I, 1905, pp. 534ff; Vol. II, 1905, pp. 97ff.

H. Duensing, *Der Aethiopische Text der Kirchenordnung des Hippolyt*, Göttingen 1946; W. Till, J. Leipoldt, *Der Koptische Text der Kirchenordnung des Hippolyt*, TUGAL 58 (1954).

Funk Vol. I, *Constitutiones Apostolorum* VII (p. 534) :

XXXII :   Those that first come to the mystery of godliness (εὐσέβεια) let them be brought to the bishop or to the presbyters by the deacons and let them be examined ... and let those that bring them exactly inquire about their character ... let their manners (οἱ τρόποι) and life be inquired into ...

Funk Vol. II, p. 107f. XII : Three years let them be catechumenoi while listening to the word of learning.

XXIII :   The catechumenoi shall pray separately and after prayer let them not kiss the believers (= full members) because their kiss is yet not pure.

XV :   When one has been chosen or prepared himself for baptizing let them be examined regarding their way of life, whether they lived with fear of God, whether they cared for widows, visited the sick and performed good deeds... When the day arrives when they are to be baptized let the bishop take them in oath to ensure that they be pure.

XIX :   The catechumenoi shall not dine together with the believers at the Lord's table.

XX :   And those invited to the table shall eat without quarrelling, furthermore when the bishop permits let them speak and ask whatever it is and he shall answer.

APPENDIX E

The Recent Monograph of Schiffman

After the completion of this study there appeared the monograph by Lawrence H. Schiffman : *Sectarian Law in the Dead Sea Scrolls : Courts, Testimony and the Penal Code,* Brown Judaic Studies 33 (Scholars Press, Chico, California), 1983. Schiffman made a thorough analysis of the legal rules in the Manual of Discipline (= 1QS) and in the Covenant of Damascus (= CD). His work is based on the supposition that the sectarian rules are the outcome of an inner development of sectarian life. Schiffman admits that the organizational rules of the sect and especially the penal code and the rules of entry and expulsion have no basis in Jewish scripture but he nevertheless argues that these rules were intended to fulfill ideals inherent in the Bible (p. 212). I, for one, cannot agree with this supposition. The evidence supplied in this study shows that the *organizational* rules of the Qumran sect have nothing to do with specific Jewish ideals. They rather reflect the way guilds and religious associations of the Hellenistic period used to structure their regulations of order. In the light of the evidence we have adduced here it seems clear that procedures of maintaining sects, clubs and guilds were identical in the ancient world. Rules about the entry of new members into the sect and about the novitiate, as well as rules about expulsion, existed in all the guilds and associations of the period in question, and therefore similar rules in the Qumran sect cannot be seen as the result of the concept of purity in Qumran, as Schiffman contends (p. 216). It is true, sectarian life in Qumran had its particular rules of purity and of course was subject to strict observance of the Torah commandments : hence the frequent allusions to purity, etc., in the sectarian rules. However these did not affect the very system of rules pertaining to membership and group discipline. Such a system of rules has no place in a code of national character, but is characteristic of sectarian life in general, as we try to show in the present work. Indeed, matters of procedure such as : examination of candidates for entry in the sect, taking them under oath to keep the laws of the sect, approval of the candidates by votes of the assembly and the registration of a member, are common both to the Qumran sect and the Hellenistic-Roman guilds and religious associations. The same applies to various rules of order in social gatherings, as for example : prohibition of loud laughter during meetings, expectorating, unproper cover, sleeping in the assembly, speaking not in turn, not sitting in fixed order, abuse of high ranking members, absence from meetings etc. All these are attested in the Qumran code as well as in the codes of associations and guilds

71

of Hellenistic-Roman period, and are inconceivable in general law applied to the population as a whole. Other rules like the obligation of mutual aid and the prohibition of applying to an outside court found in the Qumran code and in the other associations can be explained only on the basis of life in a commune.

All these have nothing to do with 'inspired biblical exegesis' as Schiffman argues (p. 39) but with conventional rules of associations determined on a voluntary basis by the members of the associations themselves (cf. above p. 24). Schiffman is right in arguing that rejecting the commands of one's superior means rejecting a sectarian decision, but his conclusion that this is tantamount to rejection of God's commands (p. 39) has no basis whatsoever. One must distinguish between divine commands sanctified by the Torah which belong to the sphere of the covenant between God and Israel, and the regulations of the sect which relate to the social organization of the sect, and as such do not apply to the people of Israel as a whole but to a specific group which is bound by rules accepted voluntarily by its members. By ignoring the universal character of sectarian organizational procedure, Schiffman tends to discover halakhic features in matters which have actually no affinities to Halakha. Thus he compares the procedure of initiation of a member of the Qumran sect to that of halakhic conversion (pp. 156-157). However there is no room at all for comparison here. The conversion ceremony includes instruction of Torah rules such as the gleanings left for the poor man (Lev. 19:9, 23:2), the forgotten sheaves (Deut. 24:19), leaving the corner of the field (Lev. 19:9, 23:2), title for the poor man (Deut. 14:28-29, 26:12-13) (TB Yebamot 47a-b), whereas the Qumran code contains only specific rules related to the life of the sect and its organization. When one finds in the Damascus covenant the obligation to help the poor it occurs there in the framework of the social welfare system of the sect (CD 14:12-16), and as indicated above this kind of obligations for mutual aid is attested in the codes of the various sects of Ptolemaic Egypt (cf. above pp. 31-34). At any rate, rules about mutual aid are not envisaged at all in the laws of the Torah; on the other hand, since they are vital in communal life they occur in the various codes of sects, clubs and associations.

In fact the whole procedure of initiation of new members into the sect has its parallels in the codes of various guilds and sects. Graded initiation accompanied by an oath as found in the Manual of Discipline (1QS 5:1ff., 6:16ff.) was a common phenomenon in the mysteries and the religious associations of the Hellenistic period. Thus, for example, we read in the *Metamorphoses* of Lucius Apuleius that Lucius was bound by an oath to the "holy order" (*sancta militia*) (XI, 15) and that he underwent probation before becoming "wholly devout to the goddess"

(XI, 19). Similarly we hear from Livy (XXXIX, 15, 13) about men of the Bacchic mysteries who were initiated by an oath of allegiance (*sacramentum*). (For a thorough investigation of this problem see R. Reitzenstein, *Die Hellenistischen Mysterienreligionen/3*, 1927, pp. 192ff., and see also my article 'The Loyalty Oath in the Ancient Near East', *Ugarit Forschungen* 8 (1976), pp. 407ff.). A procedure of initiation similar to that of Qumran is attested in the "Apostolic tradition" as recorded by Hippolytus (cf. above p. 68).

Schiffman's tendency to see every legal rule in the Qumran sect against the background of Jewish law has caused misunderstandings in two judicial concepts : "Judges" and "Reproof".

"Judges"

Schiffman understands the term *shophet* in the Qumran rules as "judge" in the strict juridical sense and therefore is surprised to find judges involved in welfare distribution (CD 14:12-16). He goes therefore into speculation and suggests (p. 38), on the basis of comparison with a passage in Philo, that the rule in the Covenant of Damascus was legislated in order to make clear that although a judge in the courtroom is not allowed to give special consideration for the poor (cf. Exod. 23:3), charity is of great importance and even the "judge" should participate in the administration of social welfare. This speculation however is unnecessary because *shophet* in the Bible as well as in Qumran is not limited to judicial function but implies legislative as well as executive function (cf. my article 'Judge and Officer in Ancient Israel and in the Ancient Near East', *Israel Oriental Studies* 7 (1977) pp. 65-88). The ten שפטי העדה in CD 10:4f. actually constitute a court as well as a legislative and administrative body of the sect and actually correspond to the Sanhedrin which is called like the Qumran sect κοινόν (Josephus, *Vita* 190, 309) or σύνοδος (BJ I:170). In my present study I therefore refer to the institution of "judges" as the *council* of the sect (above pp. 16ff.). In my opinion the group of fifteen in 1QS 8:1 is to be seen as the leadership of the sect, especially because we find a leadership of fifteen in guilds and associations of the Hellenistic-Roman period (see above p. 19). It is interesting to note that the association of the Labyads in Delphi which had a management body of fifteen (see p. 19), had a rule that 101 votes was the minimum for adopting a decision, which reminds us Josephus' account about the Essenes that a decision was adopted only with a minimum of hundred members (BJ II 145).

The proposal raised by J. Licht (cf. above p. 16, note 43) to see the group of fifteeen as a minimum number of the community cannot be accepted because this would clash with the explicit rule in 1QS 6:3 about a minimum of ten for maintaining the full order of the sect. That the fifteen are depicted as a "holy house" (בית קדש, 1QS 8:6-7) or "holy abode" (מעון קדש, 1QS 8:9-10) should not surprise us since they constitute a body which represents the sect and as such embodies the ideals of the whole congregation.

The fifteeen should be seen as the executive body of the sect (a sort of Sandhedrin) while the *môshab ha-rabbim* is to be considered an assembly responsible for fixing the rules of the sect, acceptance of new members and routine jurisdiction.

The existence of a group of leaders which carries out the decisions of the assembly is characteristic of all the sects and associations dealt with here, and as indicated above (p. 18) seems to have existed in the first Christian congregation. The three priests within the council of fifteen should be seen as presiding over the council, in accordance with the principle prevailing in the sect that the priest presides the meetings and communal meals (cf. 1QS 6:3-4, 9:7). The superior role of the priest should not be seen as the result of the veneration of Zadokite priests, as Schiffman contends (p. 215), but stems from the fact that the priest had a dominant position in all the associations of the Hellenistic period (cf. above p. 19). This principle pervaded also the Pharisaic *ḥaburah* which also had rules that the priest should be first in pronouncing the blessings at the meal etc. (Cf. the references and the discussion of Schiffman, pp. 194f.).

"Reproof"

In 1QS 6:1 and in CD 9:2 we find a rule concerning false accusation : not to bring a charge against any member which is not based on evidence by witnesses : אשר לא בתוכחת לפני עדים (1QS 6:1) or אשר לא בהוכח לפני עדים (CD 9:3). Such a charge constitutes slander which should not be tolerated in an ideal community founded on a voluntary basis. As I have shown above (pp. 38-39), identical rules are found in the codes of the religious association of the Hellenistic-Roman period. Thus we read in the Iobacchi code that the insulted member should bring two witnesses that heard the accused insulting (see above p. 39 and p. 56).

Schiffman however translates the words הוכח (CD 9:3) and תוכחת (1QS 6:1) not "proof' or 'evidence' but 'reproof' and argues that it is not 'evidence' produced by witnesses which is intended but 'reproof', the halakhic formal act of התראה "warning" accompanied by two witnesses, which had to be administered before the culprit committed the crime. This interpretation was actually raised as a possibility already by Ch. Rabin in his commentary on the Covenant of Damascus (p. 45) but was rejected by him, with the reason that Rabbinic התראת had to be made before the crime, whereas in Qumran the reproof comes after the deed (and see below).

Similarly J. Licht refers to this interpretation by saying : 'the similarity to התראה is superficial' (p. 137).

Indeed there is no room for comparison of the Qumran "reproof" with התראה (hatra'ah) at all for the following reasons :

1) *Hatra'ah* in Rabbinic literature comes to ensure that the culprit was aware of the transgression and its consequences when he committed the crime so that the execution of the punishment could be fully justified. This then has nothing to do with the commandment in Lev. 19:17-18 on which the rules of CD 9:3 and 1QS 6:1 are based. The law of Lev. 19:17-18 is of moral and not of forensic nature, i.e. it aims to avoid conflict and hatred between members of the Israelite society and in this sense it occurs in the rules of Qumran : 'to reprove each his neighbor ... with humility and lovingkindness ... but on the very day shall he reprove him lest he bear guilt because of him' (1QS 5:24-6:1). In other words the law encourages men to straighten out their conflicts with their comrades in order to avoid enmity and complaints before the court; the legal rule of *hatra'ah* on the other hand is not concerned with relationship amongst the members of a group but rather with the proper execution of punishment for crimes committed in society at large. Indeed the Rabbinic rules of *hatra'ah* are never linked to Lev. 19:17-18.

2) The *hatra'ah* in Rabbinic law had to be made before witnesses in order to prove that the culprit had been warned before he committed the crime, while according to 1QS 5:24f. quoted above one ought to reprove his neighbor first privately (compare Matt. 18:15f. and see Maimonides *Hilkhot De'ot* 6:7 quoted above p. 41, note 195). Only when the complaint is submitted to the assembly he must bring witnesses (6:1).

3) The analogy with the regulation of the guilds and especially the Iobacchi code makes clear that the aim of the law of bringing witnesses before going to court is prevention of false accusation and slander, and not a legal measure for enabling the execution of punishment, as is *hatra'ah* before witnesses. Life in a commune demands self-discipline and sincerity, therefore a member of a voluntary group should clarify matters with his feelow in the group before submitting the quarrel with him to the court. Only when this did not help, and the fellow, in spite of all, decided to go to court, will judgment take place, provided that the offended can bring witnesses to prove his accusation.

4) The basic difference between Rabbinic *hatra'ah* and Qumran הוכח / תוכחת is that *hatra'ah* is always administered before committing the crime while the 'reproof' in Qumran is done during or after committing the crime, as is the situation in the law of reproof in Lev. 19:17-18.

Indeed the overseer (מבקר) in Qumran has to record the reproof made *after* every offense (cf. CD 9:16-23). In Rabbinic law, however, the warning has to be done orally *before* the comission of the crime and only then is the person liable for conviction. This difference has been observed by Schiffman (p. 97), but it did not change his position.

Schiffman's work is most important for understanding the sectarian laws and its minutiae; hoevever, the body of sectarian rules of organizational procedure as a whole, and its particular provisions, cannot be understood unless we take in account the specific rules conditioned by the esoteric nature of the sect, and their parallels in ancient society.

SYNOPSIS
Common traits of Guilds and Associations

	Qumran 1QS, CD	Greek-Roman	Egyptian, Demotic	New Testament, Early Christian communities	Pharisaic, Rabbinic, others
I. Appelation of the sect :	סרך	τάξις σπεῖρα		—	—
	יחד	κοινόν κοινωνία	śnt (1)	ἐκκλησία κοινωνία	מחדרין כנסת חבורה
	הרבים	πλῆθος	mš'	οἱ πολλοί	הרבים
II. Number of Councillors (2) : 12 (12 12 12)(3)	12 (12 12 12)(3)	—	12 (4)	12 (12 12) (5)	12(12 12 1) (6)
	10 (7)	10 (8)	10 (9)	—	10 (10)
	—	—	—	7 (11)	7 (12)
	15	15 (13)	—	—	—
III. Titles of Officials :	כהן	ἱερεύς (magister)	wr	—	כהנא אפכלא (Nabatean)
	פקיד הרבים מבקר	ἐπιμελητής ἐπίσκοπος (curator)	mr ms'	ἐπίσκοπος	מבקרא (Nabatean)
	מבקר	ταμίας (quaestor)	mr šn	ἐπίσκοπος	כהנא

	Qumran IQS, CD	Greek-Roman	Egyptian, Demotic	New Testament, Early Christian communities	Pharisaic, Rabbinic, others
IV. Acceptance of members :					
Oath of admission	x	x	—	x (14)	x (15)
Registration	x	x	—	—	—
Examination	x	x	—	x (16)	x (17)
Decision by lot	x (גורל)	—	—	x (18)	—
Probationary period	2 years	—	10 years (19)	3 or 6 years (20)	1 year (21)
Submission of private property	x	—	x	x	—
V. Renewal of the covenant :	x	x	x	—	—
VI. Regulations and rules :					
Infidelity or rebellion	x	x	x	—	x (22)
causing disorder	x	x	x	—	x
fixed order (sitting, speaking)	x	x	x	x (23)	—
abuse of high ranking members	x	—	x	x (24)	—
abuse of member's property	x	x	x	—	x (25)
anger, mockery, cheating, arrogance	x	x	—	x (26)	—
false accusation	x	x	x	x	—
reproof of members (27)	x	—	—	x	x
causing disturbance in assembly	x	x	x	—	—
absence from assembly	x	x	x	—	—
immodesty (nudity, expectoration, extension of left hand)	x	—	—	—	—
calumny	x	—	x	x (28)	x (29)
assault	x	x	x	x (30)	x (31)
mutual aid	x	x	x	x (32)	x (33)
applying to an external court	x (CD 9:1)?	x	x	—	—
VII. Cult, worship etc. :					
sacrifices	—	x	x	—	—
communal meals (34)	x	x	x	x	x
funerary customs	—	x	x	—	—
suppliance of firewood	x (37)	x (38)	x (35)	—	—
night watch	x	—	—	—	x (36)
VIII. Penalties :					
exclusion from the Purity	x	—	—	x (39)	x (ḥaburah) (40)
temporary expulsion	x	—	—	—	—
expulsion	x	x	x	—	—
fines	—	x	x	—	—
forfeit of ration	x	—	—	—	—

NOTES TO SYNOPSIS

1 Cf. recently M. Muszynski, 'Les "associations religieuses" en Egypte', *Orientalia Lovaniensia Periodica* 8 (1977) pp. 146-147.
2 The sects adopted the structure of their leadership/courts from the organization of their national bodies, hence the identity in number of councillors in sects and state organizations.
3 Temple Scroll 57:11-13.
4 In courts of the Ramesside period, cf. above p. 18.
5 *Revelation* chap. 21, cf. above p. 17.
6 The court of twenty three, the small Sanhedrin of the Rabbinic sources, cf. above pp. 17-18.
7 CD 10:4f.
8 δεκάπρωτοι and decemprimi/decemviri in the Greek-Roman communities.
9 Cf. above p. 18, note 60.
10 Cf. Ruth 4:6; Qoheleth 7:19; Josephus *AJ* XX, 194.
11 Acts 6:1ff.
12 Josephus *BJ* II, 570; *AJ* IV, 214, 287; B. Megillah 26a.
13 πεντεκαίδεκα, cf. above, p. 19.
14 Cf. the Apostolic tradition of Hippolytus, above p. 70.
15 Enrollment in the *Ḥaburah* involves "taking upon himself" קבל עליו which is tantamonous to taking an oath (שבועה), see S. Lieberman, *JBL* 71 (1952) pp. 199-200.
16 *Apostolic Tradition* of Hippolytus and *Epistle of Peter* (Pseudo-Clementine), cf. above pp. 65-70.
17 The candidate to the *Ḥaburah* was investigated as to his behavior, cf. Tos. Demai II, 10. If he is a tax collector he cannot be admitted, cf. Tos. Demai III, 4 (cf. S. Lieberman, *JBL* 71 (1952) pp. 199f.). For restrictions of admittance for various professions of immoral or irreligious character cf. *Apostolical Constitutions* VIII, 32 (ed. F.X.Funk).
18 Cf. Acts 1:17 in connection with the choice of Mathias by casting the lots.
19 Cf. Pap. Berlin 3115, cf. above p. 44.
20 In the *Apostolic Tradition* : 3 years; in the *Epistle of Peter* (Ps.-Clementine) : 6 years.
21 Cf. Tos. Demai II, 12, see S. Lieberman *JBL* 17 (1952), p. 202.
22 Cf. above p. 42.
23 Cf. the *Apostolic Tradition* of Hippolytus, above p. 70 no. XX.
24 ibid.
25 Cf. the oath of the En-Gedi community concerning stealing property of members, above p. 58.
26 Matthew 5:22, cf. above, p. 38.
27 Cf. the discussion in Appendix E pp. 74-76.
28 Matthew 5:22.
29 Cf. the oath of the En-Gedi community, see above p. 58.
30 For care for widows in the first Christian congregation Acts 6:1-7.
31 The principle of גמלות חסדים as defined in Mishnah Peah 1:1 (cf. p. 32 n. 133) apparently has its roots in the Pharisaic *ḥaburah*.
32 I Corinthians 6:1, cf. above p. 34.
33 For Rabbinic prohibitions of recourse to pagan courts cf. B. Gittin 88b; *Midrash Tanaaim* (ed. Hoffmann) to Deut. 16-18. Furthermore one should not be judged before the *Am-Haareẓ*, cf. *Mekhilta de R. Simon bar Yohai* (ed. Epstein-Melamed) p. 158.

34 Cf. M. Delcor, 'Repas Cultuels Esséniens et Thérapeutes, Thiases et Haburoth', *RQ* 6 (1967-69), pp. 401-425.

35 Cf. above p. 50.

36 It is first attested in Neh. 10:35 (for the sectarian nature of Nehemiah's pact, see my article in *VT* 23 (1971) pp. 72ff.) and occurs later in the Temple Scroll (see Yadin *TS* I pp. 99f.) and in the Second Temple sources (Yadin, ibid., p. 100).

37 1Q6:6-7 : 'In a place where there are ten, there must not fail to be a man who studies the Torah day and night continually, relieving one another' (read עליפות = חליפות, Yalon, *Studies in the Dead Sea Scrolls* (Philological Essays), Jerusalem 1967 p. 72 (Hebrew))... they shall spend the third part of every night ... reciting from the book'. The vigils are used here for studying Torah but it seems that the necessity to keep awake and the division of the watches of the night for this purpose were conditioned by the circumstances of the sectarian life.

38 Cf. the new Attic club (cf. above p. 9, code no. 15): 'Let them establish three powerful men as nightwatchmen...'

39 Cf. the *Apostolic Tradition* of Hippolytus XIX, above p. 70 : ... : 'The cate- chumenoi shall not dine together with the believers at the Lord's table'. Compare also XIII there.

40 Cf. Tos. Demai II, 2; Mishnah Demai II, 3 and see Ch. Rabin, *Qumran Studies* pp. 12ff.

Selected Bibliography

J. Allegro, "Further Messianic References in Qumran Literature", *JBL* 75 (1956) 174-187.

G. Alon, *Meḥqarim be-Toledot Israel* 2 vol., Tel Aviv, 1967-1970 (Hebrew).

H. Bardtke, "Die Rechtsstellung der Qumran-Gemeinde", *ThLZ* 86 (1961) 93-101.

J. Baumgarten, "The Duodecimal Courts of Qumran, the Apocalypse and the Sanhedrin", *JBL* 95 (1976), 52-78.

I.F. Baer, "Serek Hayaḥad", *Zion* 29 (1964) 35ff (Hebrew).

A. Berliner, *Randbemerkungen zum täglichen Gebetbuch*, Berlin, 1969.

M. Beer, "The Emergence of the Talmudic Academy in Babylonia", *Proceedings of the Fourth World Congress of Jewish Studies*, I (1967), 98-101.

M. Black, *An Aramaic Approach to the Gospels and Acts*, Oxford, 3rd ed., 1966.

F. de Cenival, *Les Associations religieuses en Egypte d'après les documents démotiques*, Caire, 1972.

R.M. Charles, *The Greek Versions of the Testaments of the Twelve Patriarchs*, Oxford, 1968.

H. Conzelmann, *I Corinthians (Hermeneia Series)*, Philadelphia, 1975.

F.M. Cross, *The Ancient Library of Qumran*, N.Y., 1961.

F. Cumont, "La grande inscription bacchique", *American Journal of Archaeology* 37 (1933), 232ff.

M. Delcor, "Repas cultuels esséniens et thérapeutiques et ḥaburoth", *Revue de Qumran* 4 (1968), 401-425.

W. Dittenberger, *Sylloge Inscriptionum Graecarum*, Leipzig, 1898-1901.

H. Donner, W. Röllig, *Kanaanäische und Aramäische Inschriften*, 1-3, Wiesbaden, 1964.

E. Drerup, "Ein antikes Vereinsstatut", *Neue Jahrbücher für Klass. Altertum* III (1899), 356-370.

A. Dupont-Sommer, *Nouveaux aperçus sur les manuscrits de la Mer Morte*, Paris, 1953.

L. Edelstein, *The Hippocratic Oath*, Baltimore, 1943.

W. Erichsen, *Die Satzungen einer ägyptischen Kultgenossenschaft aus der Ptolemäerzeit* (=Pap. Prague), Copenhagen, 1959.

J.A. Fitzmeyer, *Essays on the Semitic Background of the New Testament,* London, 1971.

D. Flusser, 'The Pesher of Isaiah and the Twelve Apostles', *Eretz-Israel* 8 (1966-67), 52-62.

F.X. Funk, *Didascalia et Constitutiones Apostolorum* Vol. I-II, Paderbornae, 1905.

Th. Gaster, *The Dead Sea Scriptures,* Engl. translation N.Y., 1957.

L. Ginsberg, *An Unknown Jewish Sect* (translated from the German edition of 1922), N.Y., 1976.

J. Greenfield, "The Marzeaḥ as a Social Institution", *Acta Antiqua Academiae Hungaricae* 22 (1974), 451-455.

E. Haenchen, *The Acts of the Apostles : A Commentary,* Philadelphia, Westminster, 1971.

M. Hengel, "Qumran und der Hellenismus", *Qumran, sa piété, sa théologie et son milieu,* Paris-Leuven (ed. M. Delcor), 1978.

A. Herdner, *Corpus des tablettes en cunéiformes alphabétiques découvertes à Ras Shamra-Ugarit de 1929 à 1939,* Paris, 1963 (=CTA).

R. Hanhart, *Text und Textgeschichte des I Esrabuches,* Göttingen, 1974.

H. Hunger, *Babylonische und assyrische Kolophone* (AOAT 2), Neukirchen, 1967.

A. Hurvitz, *The Transition Period in Biblical Hebrew,* Jerusalem, 1972 (Hebrew).

Husselman, Boak, Edgerton, *Papyri from Tebtunis,* Michigan, 1944.

W.H.J. Jones, *The Doctor's Oath,* Cambridge, 1924.

W.H.J. Jones, *Hippocrates* I-II (Loeb Classical Library), London, 1923.

M.Z. Kaddari, *Semantic Fields in the Language of the Dead Sea Scrolls,* Jerusalem, 1968 (Hebrew).

S.A. Kaufman, *The Akkadian Influence on Aramaic,* Assyriological Studies 19, Chicago, London, 1974.

S.S. Kottek, J.O. Leibowitz, O. Richler, "A Hebrew Paraphrase of the Hippocratic Oath" (15th Cent. Manuscript), *Medical History* 22 (1978) 438-445.

B. Levine, "Aramaic Texts from Persepolis", *JAOS* 92 (1972), 70-79.

J. Licht, *Megillat HaSerakhim,* Jerusalem, 1965 (Hebrew).

S. Lieberman, "The Discipline in the so-called Dead Sea Manual of Discipline", *JBL* 71 (1952), 199-206.

S. Lieberman, *Tosephta ki-Peshutah,* New York, 1955-

S. Lieberman, "A Preliminary Remark on the Inscription of En-Gedi", *Tarbiz* 40 (1970), 25-26.

J. Licht, "Legs as a Sign of Election", *Tarbiz* 35 (1961), 18-24 (Hebrew).

B. Lifschitz, *Donateurs et fondateurs dans les synagogues juives,* 1964.
B. Lifschitz, "The Ancient Synagogue of Hamath-Tiberias, its Floor and Inscription", *Studies in the History of the Jewish People and the Land of Israel,* Vol. 3, ed. Oded, Rappaport, Schochat, Schatzmiller, Haifa, 1974, 99-109.
S.F. Loewenstamm, "From this Time forth and Forevermore", *Tarbiz* 32 (1963) 313-316 (Hebrew).
P.M. Lurje, *Studien zum altaegyptischen Recht,* 1971.

A. Malamat, "Mari and the Bible : Some Patterns of Tribal Organization and Institutions", *JAOS* 82 (1962), 144-150.
B. Mazar, "The Philistines and the Rise of Israel and Tyre", *Proceedings of the Israel Academy of Arts and Sciences,* vol. I, no. 7 (1964), 19ff.
B. Mazar, "The Inscription on the Floor of the Synagogue in En-Gedi Preliminary Survey", *Tarbiz* 40 (1970), 18-23.
H. Mantel, "The Nature of the Great Synagogue" *HThR* 60 (1967), 68-91.
J.T. Milik, *Dédidaces Faites par des Dieux, Recherches d'Epigraphie Proche-Orientale* I, 1972.
J. Murphy-O'Connor, "La genèse littéraire de la Règle de la Communauté", *RB* 76 (1979), 528-540.

J. Naveh, *On Stone and Mosaic,* The Aramaic and Hebrew Inscriptions from Ancient Synagogues, Jerusalem, 1978 (Hebrew).
J. Naveh, "Some Notes on Nabatean Inscriptions from 'Avdat" *IEJ* 17 (1967), 187-189.
A. Negev, "Nabatean Sanctuary at Jebel Moneijah", *IEJ* 27 (1977) 211-231.
A. Negev, "Nabatean Inscriptions from 'Avdat (Oboda)" *IEJ* 13 (1963) 113-124.
J. Neusner, "ḤBR and N'MN", *RQ* 5 (1964-66), 119-122.
F. Nötscher, *Zur Theologischen Terminologie der Qumran-Texte,* Bonn, 1956.

S. Pines, "The Oath of Asaph the Physician and Yohanan ben Zabda", *Proceedings of the Israel Academy of Science and Humanities* V (1975) 223-262.
F. Poland, *Geschichte des griechischen Vereinswesens,* Leipzig, 1909.
H.J. Polotsky, "Three Greek Documents from the Family Archive of Babatha" *EI* 8 (1967), 46-51.

G. Quandt, *De Baccho ab Alexandri aetate in Asia Minore culto,* Halle, 1912.

Ch. Rabin, *The Zadokite Documents,* Oxford, 1954.

Ch. Rabin, *Qumran Studies,* Oxford, 1957.

N. Rhodokanakis, *Altsabäische Texte,* I (SBWA Phil.-Hist. Klasse 206) 1927.

U. Rappaport, "On the Meaning of Heber Ha-Yehudim", *Studies in the History of the Jewish People and the Land of Israel,* vol. 3 (eds. Oded, Rappaport-Schochet-Schatzmiller) Haifa, 1974, 59-67 (Hebrew).

A.E. Raubitschek, "A New Attic Club (ERANOS)", *The J. Paul Getty Museum Journal* ((1981), 93-98.

B. Rehm, *Die Pseudoklementinen, Homilien I* (Die Griech.-Christl. Schriftsteller 42) 1953.

R. Reitzenstein, *Die hellenistischen Mysterienreligionen,* 3rd ed., Leipzig, 1927.

F. Rosenthal, *A Grammar of Biblical Aramaic,* Wiesbaden, 1963.

C.H. Roberts, T.C. Skeat and A.D. Nock, "The Guild of Zeus Hypsistos", *HThR* 29 (1936), 39-88.

M. San Nicolo, *Aegyptisches Vereinswesen zur Zeit der Ptolemäer und Römer* II, München, 1915.

M. San Nicolo, "Zur Vereinsgerichtsbarkeit im Hellenistischen Aegypten", *Epitymbion, Festschrift für H. Swoboda,* Reichenberg 1927, 255-300.

S. Schechter, *Saadyana,* Cambridge, 1903.

S. Schechter, *Fragments of a Zadokite Work,* cf. now *Documents of Jewish Sectaries* 2 vols. in 1 with "Prolegomenon" by J.A. Fitzmyer N.Y., KTAV, 1970.

L.H. Schiffman, *The Halakhah at Qumran,* 1975.

L.H. Schiffman, *Sectarian Law in the Dead Sea Scrolls,* Courts, Testimony and the Penal Code, Chico, 1983.

E. Seidl, *Einführung in die ägyptische Rechtsgeschichte bis zum Ende des neuen Reiches,* I, Juristischer Teil, third ed. Glückstadt-Hamburg-N.Y., 1956.

E. Seidl, *Ptolemäische Rechtsgeschichte,* second revised ed. Glückstadt-Hamburg-N.Y., 1962.

K. Sethe, J. Partsch, *Demotische Urkunden zum ägyptischen Burgschaftsrechte vorzüglich der Ptolemäerzeit,* Leipzig, 1920.

C. Schneider, "Zur Problematik des Hellenistischen in den Qumrantexten", *Qumranprobleme,* ed. H. Bardtke, 1963, 299-344.

G. Strecker, *Das Judenchristentum in den Pseudoklementinen,* Texte und Untersuchungen zur Geschichte der altchristlichen Literatur, 70, 1958.

S. Talmon, "The Sectarian יחד — a Biblical Noun", *VT* 3 (1953) 133-140.

M.J. Teixidor, "Le Thiase de Belastre et de Beelshamèn", CRAIBL Avril-Juin 1981, 306-314.

R.C. Thompson, *Assyrian Medical Texts*, London/N.Y. 1923.

W. Till, J. Leipoldt, *Der Koptische Text der Kirchenordnung des Hippolyt*, TU 58 (1954).

E.E. Urbach, *The Sages*, Jerusalem, 1975.

E.E. Urbach, "Courts of Twenty-three", *Proceedings of the 5th World Congress of Jewish Studies*, Section 2, 1972, 37-48.

E.E. Urbach, "The Secret of the En-Gedi Inscription and its Formula", *Tarbiz*, 40 (1970), 27-30.

J.P. Waltzing, *Etude historique sur les corporations professionnelles chez les Romains* I-IV, 1895.

E. Weidner, "Hof- und Harems-erlasse assyrischer Könige etc." *Archiv. für Orientforschung* 17 (1954-56), 257-293.

M. Weinfeld, "The Council of the Elders to Rehoboam", *Maarav, A Journal for the Study of the North-West Semitic Languages and Literatures*, 2 (1982), 27-53.

M. Weinfeld, "The Loyalty Oath in the Ancient Near East", *UF* 8 (1976), 379-414.

M. Weinfeld, "Judge and Officer in Ancient Israel and in the Ancient Near East", *Israel Oriental Studies* 7 (1977), 231-253.

M. Weinfeld, *Justice and Righteousness in Israel and the Nations in the Light of Social Reforms in the Ancient Near East*, Jerusalem, 1985.

M. Weinfeld, "The Spiritual Metamorphosis of Israel in the Jeremian Prophecy", *ZAW* 88 (1976), 17-56.

M. Weinfeld, *Deuteronomy and the Deuteronomic School*, Oxford, 1972.

M. Weinfeld, "The Origin of the Apodictic Law — An Overlooked Source", *VT* 23 (1973), 63-75.

M. Weinfeld, "The Genuine Jewish Attitude Towards Abortion", *Zion* 42 (1978) (Hebrew), 129-142.

P. Wernberg-Moeller, *The Manual of Discipline*, Leiden, 1957.

A.J. Wertheimer, *Batei Midrashot*, Jerusalem, 1968 (Hebrew).

D.B. Weisberg, *Guild Structure and Political Allegiance in Early Achaemenid Mesopotamia*, New-Haven, 1967.

H.A. Wolfson, *Philo*, Foundations of Religious Philosophy in Judaism, Christianity and Islam, I-II, Cambridge, Massachusetts. Fourth printing revised, 1968.

Y. Yadin, *The Scroll of the War of the Sons of Light against the Sons of Darkness*, Oxford, 1962.

Y. Yadin, *The Temple Scroll*, Jerusalem, 1983 (English).

H. Yalon, *Studies in the Dead Sea Scrolls* (Philological Essays 1949-1952) Jerusalem, 1967 (Hebrew).

H.C. Youtie, "The *Kline* of Sarapis", *HThR* 41 (1948), 9-29.

C. Ziebarth, *Das Griechische Vereinswesen*, Leipzig, 1896.

Abbreviations

BS	Ben Sira
CD	Covenant of Damascus
CRAIBL	Comptes rendus de l'Académie des Inscriptions et Belles Lettres
CTA	Corpus de tablettes en cunéiforme alphabétique (A. Herdner)
DJD	Discoveries of the Judean Desert
EI	Eretz Israel (published by Israel Exploration Society)
HThR	Harvard Theological Review
IEJ	Israel Exploration Journal
JAOS	Journal of the American Oriental Society
JNES	Journal of Near Eastern Studies
KAI	Donner and Röllig, Kanaanäische und Aramäische Inschriften
M	(Milḥamah) War Scroll of Qumran
S	(Serekh) Manual of Discipline
JBL	Journal of Biblical Literature
RB	Revue Biblique
RQ	Revue de Qumran
SVT	Supplement to Vetus Testamentum
ThLZ	Theologische Literaturzeitung
ThWAT	Theologisches Wörterbuch zum Alten Testament
UF	Ugarit-Forschungen
VT	Vetus Testamentum
ZAW	Zeitschrift für die alttestamentliche Wissenschaft
ZNW	Zeitschrift für die neutestamentliche Wissenschaft

INDEXES

I am indebted to G.Markus and M.Benovitch for their help in preparing the bibliography and the indices.

CD — Damascus Covenant
1:9ff	45
1:11	45n224
2:18	58
3:11-12	24n91
6:20ff	32, 49
7:1-2	42n200
7:2	40, 49
8:5	42n200
8:19	24n91
9:1	34n150
9:2	74
9:2-4	38
9:3	74, 75
9:6	40n194
9:6-8	40, 49
9:9-10	34n152
9:16-23	76
9:24	57
10:4f	18, 73, 79
10:9ff	47
10:18	31n129
11:14	27
12:8	11n7, 14n31
12:19,22	11n11
13:4	48
13:9	20, 21
13:11	22
13:11-12	55
13:12	23n86, 48
13:15	10n6, 14n31
14:4	23n86
14:4ff	27
14:10	26, 56
14:11	48
14:12ff	49
14:12-16	31f, 72, 73
14:16	14n31
14:17	11n11
14:20	48
14:20-21	30
20:2-8	24

1QM — War Scroll
1QM	11
2:1	10n4
2:1-3	17
2:6	10n4
5:3	12
7:1	10n4, 11n12, 12
13:1	11n12

Temple Scroll
57:11-13	17, 17n50, 79n3

Other Scrolls
4Q Ordinances 159
    16n44, 17, 17n47n48
4Q 164 (Pesher on Isaiah) 17
4Q PB 6   7n1
4QPNah III:7   7n1
Pesher on Ps. 37 45

Papyri (see also Authors, Cenival,
    Dittenberger, San Nicolo,
    Roberts-Skeat-Nock)

Pap. Berlin 3115
    25, 29n113, 43, 44, 79n19

Pap. Cairo 30605
    32n136, 34n147, 35, 37n174

Pap. Cairo 30606
    32n136, 36n162n163n171,
    37n174, 41n199

Pap. Cairo 30619
    32n136

Pap. Cairo 31179
    35n158, 36n162n163, 37n174,
    41n199

Iobacchi Code
    20,21f, 25n93, 26n102, 27, 28,
    33n146, 35n155, 37, 39, 49,
    51ff.

Labyads, code of
    39n191 (see also Labyads)

Pap. Lille 29
    26f, 32n136, 34n147, 35n158,
    38f, 41n199

Pap. London 2710
    25n96, 29, 30n121, 34n148,
    35n155, 37, 62

Pap. Michigan 243
    14n35, 27n107, 30n121,
    33n140n141n143n144n146

Pap. Praque
    25n93, 32n136, 34n147, 35n158,
    36n162n165n166n167n169n171,
    37n174,41n199

Words

This study tries to show that the organizational pattern of the Qumran sect as well as the penal code of this sect are congruent with those of the cultic associations of Ptolemaic Egypt and of other regions of the Hellenistic and Roman world. Matters of procedure such as: examination of the candidates for entry in the sect, approval of the candidate by the votes of the assembly and the registration of a member are common both to the Qumran sect and the Hellenistic-Roman guilds and associations. The same applies to various rules of order in social gatherings, as for example: prohibition of disturbances during meetings, unproper cover, sleeping in the assembly, speaking not in turn, not sitting in fixed order, abuse of high ranking members, absence from meetings etc. All these are attested in the Qumran code as well as in the codes of associations and guilds of the Hellenistic and Roman periods.

Common features are also found in the sphere of ethics and morality such as: mutual aid, the prohibition of applying to a court outside of the sect and reproof of a member in sincerity. Regulations about expulsion from the sect, absolute or temporary, and the fixing of a period of probation for each candidate are also common to the Qumran sect and the contemporary guilds.

A similar organizational pattern is to be discerned in the early Christian congregation as reflected in the New Testament and in the apostolic traditions of Hippolytus.

All these formalities common to the religious guilds and associations of the Hellenistic and Roman period do not affect the nature of the Judaeo-Christian sects which was altogether different from its contemporaneous sects.

ISBN 3-7278-0363-0 (Universitätsverlag)
ISBN 3-525-53901-0 (Vandenhoeck & Ruprecht)